JACK
LONDON
AND THE
KLONDIKE
GOLD RUSH

JACK LONDON
AND THE
KLONDIKE GOLD RUSH

Peter Lourie

WITH ILLUSTRATIONS BY
Wendell Minor

Christy Ottaviano Books
HENRY HOLT AND COMPANY
NEW YORK

Henry Holt and Company
Publishers since 1866
175 Fifth Avenue
New York, New York 10010
mackids.com

Library of Congress Cataloging-in-Publication Data
Names: Lourie, Peter, author. | Minor, Wendell, illustrator.
Title: Jack London and the Klondike gold rush / Peter Lourie, with illustrations
  by Wendell Minor.
Description: First edition. | New York : Henry Holt and Company, 2017.
Identifiers: LCCN 2016012053 (print) | LCCN 2016027771 (ebook) | ISBN 9780805097573
  (hardback) | ISBN 9780805097580 (Ebook)
Subjects: LCSH: London, Jack, 1876–1916—Juvenile literature. | Authors, American—20th
  century—Biography—Juvenile literature. | Adventure and adventurers—United States—
  Biography—Juvenile literature. | Klondike River Valley (Yukon)—Gold discoveries—
  Juvenile literature. | BISAC: JUVENILE NONFICTION / Biography & Autobiography /
  Literary. | JUVENILE NONFICTION / Adventure & Adventurers.
Classification: LCC PS3523.O46 Z6144 2017 (print) | LCC PS3523.O46 (ebook) | DDC 813/.52
  [B]—dc23
LC record available at https://lccn.loc.gov/2016012053

Our books may be purchased in bulk for promotional, educational, or business use.
Please contact your local bookseller or the Macmillan Corporate and Premium Sales Department
at (800) 221-7945 ext. 5442 or by e-mail at MacmillanSpecialMarkets@macmillan.com.

First Edition—2017 / Designed by Anna Booth
Printed in the United States of America by LSC Communications US, LLC (Lakeside Classic),
Harrisonburg, Virginia

10 9 8 7 6 5 4 3 2 1

It was in the Klondike I found myself.
There nobody talks. Everybody thinks.
You get your true perspective. I got mine.

—JACK LONDON

He was an adventurer and man of action
as few writers have ever been.

—GEORGE ORWELL

He was a fighter. He was a terrific competitor.
He wanted to win whatever he did. . . . At the same
time, while he was physically tough, he was emotionally
sensitive. He could cry over the death of his favorite
animal, or over the tragic episode in a novel.

—EARLE LABOR

BIOGRAPHER AND CURATOR
JACK LONDON MUSEUM
SHREVEPORT, LOUISIANA

CONTENTS

PART FOUR

December 3, 1897–Late January 1898: Henderson and the Creeks

PART FIVE

March–July 1898: Heading Home Down the Long Yukon River

HOME

1898–1899

DEDICATION AND GRATITUDE

To David Neufeld, Earle Labor, and Dawne Mitchell, without whom I never would have written this book. And a special thank-you to Karl Gurcke, as well as Whit Bond, the grandson of Stampeder Louis Bond, who befriended Jack London when he arrived in Dawson.

Thank you also to Steve Shaffer, Jack London's step-great-nephew, who, with his cousin Brian Shepard, now manages Jack's ranch and vineyards in Glen Ellen, California.

INTRODUCTION

Jack London headed north to strike it rich in the Klondike. At twenty-one he was among the hundreds of thousands of Stampeders, as they came to be known, who left their dull and dreary lives all over the globe in order to make a dangerous journey into the heart of Canada's Yukon Territory. Between 1896 and 1899, forty thousand gold seekers, after months of grueling travel, arrived in the gold-rush town of Dawson on the banks of the Klondike and Yukon Rivers. A mere four thousand would actually strike gold.

Jack had decided very early on that he wanted to be a writer. He loved books, was good at writing, and desperately wanted to escape the hard work of his poor childhood. If he could strike it rich, Jack would devote his life to being an author. That was his dream.

During Jack London's time, the United States was gripped in an economic depression, and jobs were scarce. Although the typical wage was only ten cents an hour, Jack was not afraid of hard work. In order to make money for his struggling family in Oakland, California—across the bay from San Francisco—he had labored with his hands from the age of six. He helped his father grow vegetables to sell. At eleven he ran two paper routes, one before and one after school. He was up by three in the morning every day, and on weekends he worked in the bowling alley, setting up pins. When Jack was fourteen, he spent ten hours a day canning pickles to bring home a dollar. Once, he worked in the cannery for thirty-six hours straight.

Lack of money forced him to drop out after only one semester at the University of California at Berkeley, and he got a job working in a laundry shop. He always wrote in his spare time and vowed to himself he'd write at least one thousand words a day—four typed, double-spaced pages. Writing steadily for the next twenty years, he would manage to produce more than two hundred short stories, as well as scores of novels and works of nonfiction. When he died at the age of forty, he had written more than fifty books, an output far greater than most writers.

From his early travels to the Klondike, Jack brought back the precious seeds of tales that bloomed into famous novels, such as *White Fang* and *The Call of the Wild*, and short stories, including "To Build a Fire" and "The White Silence." Many believe his greatest works come from his experiences on that Klondike journey of 1897–98—narratives set in the Yukon wilderness.

Although he found little gold in the creeks, Jack London nevertheless became the first American writer of the twentieth century to earn a million dollars from his writing. He died one of the world's most famous writers.

This is the story of Jack London's journey in the gold fields of the Klondike—and what he discovered there.

TRAVEL ROUTES TO
THE KLONDIKE

CHUKCHI SEA

BEAUFORT SEA

Nome

Yukon River

St. Michael

ALASKA

NORTHWEST
TERRITORIES

BERING SEA

Anchorage

Dawson

SEE
MAP
DETAIL

ALL
CANADIAN
ROUTE

YUKON
TERRITORY

GULF OF
ALASKA

Dyea

Skagway

Juneau

SKAGWAY/DYEA
ROUTE

ALBERTA

CANADA

WATER ROUTE

BRITISH
COLUMBIA

Edmonton

PACIFIC
OCEAN

N

VANCOUVER
ISLAND

Vancouver

500 MILES

Seattle

USA

WASHINGTON

Map Detail

DAWSON

Klondike River

Bonanza Creek
Eldorado Creek

STEWART

White
River

Stewart River

Pelly River

Yukon
River

Lake Laberge

Whitehorse
Rapids

Lake Bennett

Miles
Canyon

Lake Lindeman

TAGISH

Chilkoot Trail

White Pass
Trail

DYEA

SKAGWAY

Lynn Canal

JACK LONDON

AND THE

KLONDIKE GOLD RUSH

PART ONE

AUGUST 7–SEPTEMBER 8, 1897

FROM THE COAST OF ALASKA OVER
THE MOUNTAINS TO LAKE LINDEMAN

DYEA BEACH ALASKA

The mudflats at Dyea during the Stampede
(University of Washington Libraries, Special Collections, Hegg 54)

THE TRAIL BEGINS

IN **A HEAVY DRIZZLE,** Jack London and his gold-mining partners sat in dugout canoes loaded with five tons of supplies as Sitka Tlingit paddlers drove their seventy-five-foot-long boats through heavy seas. Clouds tumbled like ghosts over the craggy peaks above them. Jack had traveled a long way—first by steamer from San Francisco, California, to Juneau, Alaska, and now by wooden canoe to the coastal village of Dyea (pronounced Die-EE), Alaska, one hundred miles north of Juneau. Formerly a small Tlingit settlement, Dyea had become a raucous boomtown of wooden and canvas shanties with tenderfoot miners trying to get organized for a trek over the Coast Mountains to look for gold.

Under the scowling gray sky, wide-beamed sailing dinghies and flat-bottomed craft ran men and cargo from steamers anchored a few miles offshore to the wide mudflats at Dyea. Horses, cattle, and dogs were sometimes pitched overboard to swim to shore, where masses of freight and baggage were dumped like garbage in chaotic heaps.

When the two canoes hit ground on August 7, 1897, Jack and his partners, along with the Tlingit paddlers and their families, jumped into the icy water and pitched gear onto the flats.

With the seawater above his knees, Jack worked furiously. At five feet seven inches tall and weighing 160 pounds, Jack was fierce and muscular. He had to work fast because it was low tide, and soon the water would rise and sweep everything away. So the curly-haired, gray-eyed lad muscled his cargo out of the boat and then more than a mile down the flats to higher ground.

In order to separate his and his partners' thousands of pounds of gear from the supplies of all the other miners, Jack strained under the weight of axes, shovels, pans, cold weather clothes, stoves, and tents, along with one-hundred-pound sacks of rice, flour, sugar, bacon, and, of course, endless cans or crates of tinned beans. Beans, bacon, and bread—the three Bs—were the staples of the Stampeder, food that he and his partners would live on for a year while they hunted for gold in the Klondike.

On the beach, wild-eyed men desperately grabbed their gear and began to sort through everything. It was a crazy open-air warehouse. Everyone was in each other's way, bumping and shoving and shouting. Jack heard loud curses against the sea wind. Dogs snarled and fought among their masters' legs.

When he finished getting all his gear organized, Jack explored the makeshift settlement of fifteen hundred tents and crude wooden buildings crammed among the coastal scrub. He passed jerrybuilt stores selling food and supplies at exorbitantly

It was chaos on the Dyea waterfront.
(Museum of History & Industry, Seattle, shs2365)

high prices. He saw saloons where miners gambled and drank until they couldn't walk. He heard rowdy men shooting into the air just for the heck of it.

Here was the start of the long trek. Here Jack and thousands of other would-be miners geared up for the trip to the Klondike gold fields, six hundred miles into the interior of the Yukon. These inexperienced miners were called *cheechakos*, the term for newcomers who were ignorant of the terrain, the weather, the animals, the culture, and the necessary survival skills for the harsh Arctic winter ahead. Many would quit along the way, but Jack was sure he'd succeed.

One problem, though, was that he had to take care of his aged brother-in-law, James Shepard, a Civil War veteran. He had promised his sister, Eliza, that he'd help her sixty-year-old husband with his outfit, too—a second entire supply of food and gear. Jack was sure he'd be the only one on the trail hauling two outfits over the mountains practically by himself. As hard as that might seem, Jack thrilled at the challenge.

After hearing news of the Yukon gold strikes, Eliza had insisted that her husband, who was keen to join the Stampede, accompany Jack to the Klondike. In fact, it was something Jack couldn't refuse because the couple was funding Jack's trip. Eliza had mortgaged their house in order to buy Jack and her husband over a ton of food and gear.

In Dyea, someone just back from the mountains looked at old Shepard, then turned to Jack and said, "You ain't gonna make it, son. It's already August. You and the rest of 'em can't get over those mountains and down the river to Dawson before the river freezes in October. You just ain't gonna make it."

Jack felt a panic like a punch to the gut. To come all this way from California and then possibly not even stake a claim on a creek!

Failure? *Not me*, thought Jack. Even with Shepard along, even if the others failed, Jack was sure he'd make it down to Dawson before freeze-up. He had proven himself many times in the face of danger. He was a winner.

At seventeen, Jack had shipped out on a sealing schooner for seven months. One night, a typhoon had whipped the Sea of Japan into a torment. Hardly any sail showed, just "bare poles,"

as sailors call it, meaning Jack could only make out the masts.
The schooner was ripping along, diving into wave after wave of
white spume as the wind tried to drive the boat under. Jack's sea
mates saw that Jack had learned quickly how to handle the tiller
of the big ship, so they went below to eat their breakfast and
left him alone to skipper that three-masted schooner single-
handedly through the fierce storm.

He could barely keep the ship from rolling over. He was terrified, but when the gale was over and he was finally relieved of duty, he felt as if he could conquer any adversity.

That was when he was seventeen, and now at twenty-one, he was even more ruggedly capable—getting to the Klondike was not a problem for Jack. Or so he thought as he went back to his piles of boxes and crates and sacks to guard them against thieves on the Dyea waterfront.

Jack knew he was in a tight race against the Arctic winter. With all the gear he had to haul up over the Coast Mountains and down the Yukon River, it would take at least two months—the rest of August, all of September, and into October—to make the trek from Dyea to Dawson, known as the City of Gold, deep in the interior of Canada's Yukon Territory.

Only the year before, a great vein of gold had been struck where the Klondike River feeds into the mighty Yukon. In August 1896, three buddies—Keish (Skookum Jim Mason), Ḵáa Goox (Dawson "Tagish" Charlie), and George Carmack—were hunting moose in the hills when they discovered gold shining "like cheese in a sandwich" on little Rabbit Creek, a stream that feeds the larger Klondike River, which in

Skookum Jim Mason (Keish) poses with children at Bonanza Creek, ca. 1898.

(National Park Service, Klondike Gold Rush National Historical Park, Candy Waugaman Collection, KLGO Library, DP-110-9028)

George Carmack with pick
(Royal BC Museum and Archives,
Image B-08421)

turn feeds into the Yukon. They quickly staked and registered their mining claims and began to extract masses of gold. Prospectors already living in the area rushed to stake other creeks nearby, but the remoteness of the region and the cruel winter conditions would prevent the bulk of the world's Stampeders from reaching the area for many months.

Over the next few years, Rabbit Creek (immediately renamed Bonanza Creek) and nearby Eldorado Creek yielded some of the richest gold deposits ever.

In mid-July 1897, a year after the initial strike, two steamers from Alaska pulled into the ports of Seattle and San Francisco. Waterfront crowds watched as the newly rich prospectors carted their gold down the gangplanks, some with wheelbarrows. Here was confirmation of all the wild rumors of gold in the Klondike that had been circulating in newspapers for the previous six months.

Like tossing gasoline onto a smoldering fire, fresh news of the Klondike strike rang out across the world, and the Stampede north was on! Secretaries, bartenders, teachers, doctors, and laborers—everyone wanted to go find some gold. As many as a hundred thousand people set out for the Arctic, some of them bankrolled by investors in towns like El Paso, Texas; New York; and the capital cities of Europe—Berlin, London, and Paris.

In an August 20, 1897, article titled "Missing Long Island Boys," one newspaper reported that two thirteen-year-olds wanted to get their own gold and were planning to stop at the Central Park Zoo along the way "to see the animals."

Like everyone else in the San Francisco Bay area, Jack read about the Yukon and the arrival of the steamship in the *San Francisco Call* on July 15, 1897:

GOLD FROM THE YUKON RIVER

Half a Million Dollars' Worth of Dust Comes by the Excelsior.

One of the Miners Has Over $40,000 to Show for a Year's Work.

Among All the Steamer's Passengers Not One Has Less Than $3000 To His Credit.

The Excelsior *leaves San Francisco for the Klondike. July 28, 1897.*
(University of Washington Libraries, Special Collections UW14504)

A mere ten days later, with their "outfit" of thousands of pounds of food, clothes, and mining gear, Jack and Shepard boarded an overloaded steamer heading north. They and thousands of others were among the first Stampeders to the Yukon. The newspapers often referred to them as "Argonauts," harkening back to the Greek heroes who accompanied Jason on his quest for the Golden Fleece.

Jack also heard the disturbing news that veteran prospectors already living in the Yukon had claimed all the good areas along the creeks and rivers. People said it would be difficult to find a section of a creek to look for gold.

On board the overloaded steamer from San Francisco to

Seattle and then aboard another rust-bucket steamer to Juneau, Alaska—where they glided along with glacier-packed peaks in the background and porpoises and killer whales alongside—Jack and Shepard formed an important partnership with three other Stampeders. Since his old brother-in-law was fairly useless, Jack thought it would be wise to connect with younger men with varying skills that would allow them to pool their talents and gear (they could take only one tent, for instance), making it more possible to achieve the goal of reaching the Klondike.

They partnered up with "Big Jim" Goodman, an experienced logger and miner in his forties with a close-cropped beard and mustache; bantamweight Merritt Sloper, shorter than Jack, a little bit older, and a master carpenter and boatbuilder just back from adventures in South America; and red-whiskered Fred Thompson, like Goodman also in his forties, a tall and tidy man, who talked a lot and was a court reporter from Santa Rosa, California. Thompson said he would keep a diary of their journey to the Klondike. Big Jim had prospected in the western states of the USA and knew real gold when he saw it.

To reach the Klondike, they'd first hike the Chilkoot Trail, which was the main access route from the coast to the Yukon gold fields. The Chilkoot was a rugged thirty-three-mile trading route from Dyea through the Coast Mountains, up to Lake Lindeman and Lake Bennett in British Columbia, Canada. It was a major route for the Tlingit, Tagish, Hän, and other First Nations groups in the area. (In Canada, Native Americans are called First Nations people.)

After the Chilkoot, they'd have to build a boat (Merritt

Sloper's job); then navigate rapids, lakes, and rivers for more than 550 miles (Jack would be skipper); then begin to mine the creeks (Jim Goodman's expertise would come in handy). Fred Thompson "was the business man. When it comes to business and organization he's boss." It was a good mix of talented men and boded well for their success. The only problem was Shepard, who complained about aches and pains from the very start.

Back in Juneau, Jack had heard so many frightening stories about the trail ahead that it must have been difficult to know what to believe, except that every story seemed to warn of unbelievable troubles at the Chilkoot summit.

In order to avoid the overloaded and often delayed steamers in Juneau, Jack had hired paddlers with two seventy-five-foot-long Tlingit dugout canoes to take all their gear the one hundred miles to Dyea. The paddlers brought along their wives, babies—dogs even—and they traveled for two days, a trip Jack later described as taking him "between mountains which formed a Yosemite Valley. . . . Glaciers and waterfalls on every side."

NOW, TO BEGIN THE JOURNEY from Dyea, Jack bought a boat for ten dollars to haul his and his partners' five tons of equipment up the course of the swift Dyea River that tumbled down the mountain valley. The boat would save at least a few miles of backbreaking carries.

Jack, Shepard, Sloper, Goodman, and Thompson loaded up their little boat and threw their backs into the ropes, inching the vessel up the swift current. Occasionally, Jack spotted the snow-spiked peaks above. The ghosting and sinister fog would clear for only a second, and suddenly a massive rock face towered over hundreds of Stampeders camping everywhere on both sides of the speedy stream. Jack noticed that it was little Sloper who had the most drive. He quietly worked harder than the rest. His wiry frame, just over a hundred pounds perhaps, strained hour after hour and with no complaints out of his mouth. Recently, he had wandered through South America, working with his hands as a carpenter, and he seemed to have learned a great deal of quiet wisdom from his travels. His silent industriousness impressed young Jack.

Whenever a miner's boat overturned in the swift stream, all hope for finding gold was instantly dashed. Jack hiked past

Stampeders ford the Dyea River
with a cart full of supplies on the Chilkoot Trail, Alaska, 1897.
(University of Washington Libraries, Special Collections, La Roche 2010)

disappointed men slumped over their battered and broken boats, their heads drooping into their hands, defeated even before they had begun to hike the dreaded Chilkoot.

It took Jack and the others three days and three boatloads to haul their gear a mere four miles. Finally, they offloaded the last of it at what was known as Head of Canoe Navigation, and were as ready as ever to pack over the trail. If they got to the summit soon, it might be passable. Even now, Jack heard, it was a veritable wall of mud and cold rain. Increasingly, too, there were bouts of snow up there. True or not true, reports of Stampeders dying up ahead filtered back along the trail, and many men grew fearful.

One day, Jack heard that a blizzard—it was then late August—had swept over the summit, taking the ragged Stampeders by surprise. But down on the lower part of the trail, Jack was busy with other perils.

CHEECHAKO

LUGGING HEAVY LOADS of gear required heaps of food to relieve Jack's raging hunger. He had never eaten so many beans, so much bacon and sourdough bread. At first his stomach rebelled and couldn't keep anything down, but a few days up the trail it quieted, and he ate ravenously.

At the beginning of the Chilkoot, he and his companions hiked over sand and gravel. They maneuvered up and down the uneven trail, around boulders, through stands of cottonwood, spruce, and birch trees. They followed the canyon wall along the icy stream through thickets of alder and willow. Some days, Goodman, who was an expert tracker and hunter, left camp to roam the hills above, looking for mountain sheep and other game.

Tlingit fishermen sold ten-pound salmon and three-pound trout to the Stampeders for twenty-five cents a fish. Men with

Klondikers packing supplies on the Chilkoot Trail near Sheep Camp
(University of Washington Libraries, Special Collections, La Roche 10042)

horses and mules passed Jack as he panted like a dog on the trail. Jack lifted his aching and sweat-stained eyes to see the pack-horses suffering because the men hadn't cinched their loads on tight enough. The much-too-heavy loads were balanced unevenly on wet blankets, and the beasts suffered sore backs. Jack winced when he heard the horses groan under their huge packs as they went by him on the crowded trail. Sloper bumped into him, but Jack held his tongue.

Some of the cheechakos were able to hire native packers to help get their gear to the summit thirteen miles ahead. During this early part of the gold rush, these porters charged only eight cents a pound to pack goods, but a year later, the cost would soar to fifty cents per pound and even up to a dollar per pound for taking an outfit over the top.

Jack had no money to hire porters or buy horses. His first loads of food and equipment were sixty pounds. Shepard could barely carry forty pounds. As young Jack grew stronger and got the hang of it, he discovered the key to climbing was to make short spurts and to pace himself. He learned the native people's tump strap method of carrying heavy loads, using one long strap, wide at the center for shifting the load to his forehead and chest. The ends of the strap held the pack against his shoulder blades, centering on the spine and leaving his hands free to carry a gun or an ax. Crossing dangerous streams this way kept Jack and his partners from drowning. If Jack were to fall into the water, he would still be able to move his arms so as not to get dragged down by the heavy load on his back.

The Dyea River and all the other mountain streams grew swift and treacherous. The frigid water rushed over slick boulders. Sometimes Jack saw moss-slimy logs lashed together floating downstream, all that remained when men with huge packs lashed to their backs had lost their balance on these logs and toppled into the freezing water. The unlucky ones who could not break free drowned.

<hr />

A FEW MONTHS after Jack made the trek, in February 1898, the North-West Mounted Police of Canada, known as the Mounties, began requiring Stampeders to carry a year's supply of food with them because the Mounties were concerned about starvation in the Yukon. It was their job to keep the Stampeders safe. In addition to food, people had to take equipment such as tents, clothing, stoves, and pots and pans. This could work out to be around two thousand pounds per person. But the important thing for the Canadian Mounties wasn't the weight of the outfits (the professional packers were the ones who were keen to weigh packs in order to charge accordingly), it was the amount of food that each Stampeder took. Checking Stampeders' supplies allowed the police to keep out anyone who might starve. They could also cut out the riffraff who lived off the proceeds of crime—people who rarely packed more than a deck of cards, dice, and maybe a pistol.

SUPPLIES FOR ONE MAN FOR ONE YEAR

The list below, taken from *The Klondike Stampede* by Tappan Adney, shows suggested equipment prospectors should gather before seeking entry into Canada at the summit of the Chilkoot Pass between 1897 and 1899. Total weight: 1 ton.

8 sacks Flour (50 lbs. each).	1 gal. Vinegar.
150 lbs. Bacon.	1 box Candles.
150 lbs. Split Pease.	25 lbs. Evaporated
100 lbs. Beans.	Potatoes.
25 lbs. Evaporated Apples.	25 lbs. Rice.
25 lbs. Evaporated Peaches.	25 Canvas Sacks.
25 lbs. Apricots.	1 Wash-Basin.
25 lbs. Butter.	1 Medicine-Chest.
100 lbs. Granulated Sugar.	1 Rubber Sheet.
1½ doz. Condensed Milk.	1 set Pack-Straps.
15 lbs. Coffee.	1 Pick.
10 lbs. Tea.	1 Handle.
1 lb. Pepper	1 Drift-Pick.
10 lbs. Salt.	1 Handle
8 lbs. Baking Powder.	1 Shovel.
40 lbs. Rolled Oats.	1 Gold-Pan.
2 doz. Yeast Cakes.	1 Axe.
½ doz. 4-oz. Beef Extract.	1 Whip-Saw
5 bars Castile Soap.	1 Hand-Saw.
6 bars Tar Soap.	1 Jack-Plane.
1 tin Matches.	1 Brace.

4 Bits, assorted, ⅜₆ to 1 in.
1 8-in. Mill File.
1 6-in. Mill File.
1 Broad Hatchet.
1 2qt. Galvanized
    Coffee-Pot.
1 Fry-Pan.
1 Package Rivets.
1 Draw-Knife.
3 Covered Pails, 4, 6,
    and 8 qt., Granite.
1 Pie-Plate.
1 Knife and Fork.
1 Granite Cup.
1 each Tea and Table
    Spoon.
1 14-in. Granite Spoon.
1 Tape-Measure.
1 1½-in. Chisel.

10 lbs. Oakum.
10 lbs. Pitch.
5 lbs. 4″ Nails.
5 lbs. 3″ Nails.
6 lbs. 2″ Nails.
200 feet ⅜-in. Rope.
1 Single Block.
1 Solder Outfit.
1 14-qt. Galvanized Pail.
1 Granite Saucepan.
3 lbs. Candlewick.
1 Compass.
1 Miner's Candlestick.
6 Towels.
1 Axe-Handle.
1 Axe-Stone.
1 Emery-Stone.
1 Sheet-Iron Stove.
1 Tent.

Just a handful of miles from the beginning of the trail, Jack looked around him. The surrounding woods seemed lifeless except for the loud croaks of ravens in the foreboding gloom. When he listened carefully, he could hear the small chirps of sparrows. He also made out the sound of gunshots on the distant mountain peaks where fellow prospectors like Goodman hunted mountain goats for food and sometimes stumbled onto grizzly bears.

OYSTER PIRATE
AND SAILOR

JACK NOW TRUDGED UPWARD through constant rain. Progress forward in the lower canyon grew torturous. Some days were unbearably wet; some were just hot. Day after day, the group hauled their goods in spurts. The terrain steepened. Jack's partners passed by each other endlessly and in silence. Jack's legs ached like never before, yet he had to keep going back down the trail to get more gear and haul it up.

The journey to the summit of the Chilkoot is sixteen and a half miles from the coast, covering an elevation rise of 3,525 feet. What starts out as a fairly gentle climb through a forested canyon turns into a nightmare climb the last half mile, with five hundred practically vertical feet to the summit.

Beyond the Chilkoot summit, it would be another ten-mile slog to the shore of Lake Lindeman, where Jack and his partners would need to chop down trees and build a boat big enough to carry themselves and all their gear 550 miles down the Yukon River to Dawson City.

But Jack couldn't think that far ahead. He devoted every ounce of aching muscle just to getting the next hundred-pound load a mile up this trail.

During some of those early days on the trail, Jack was in

Stampeders on the Chilkoot Trail approach the summit.
(Yukon Archives, James Albert Johnson fonds, 86/15, #3)

great pain. After a week, he'd lost weight and his face grew lean. At times he plodded forward, but when he went back "light" to get another load, his feet dragged. Like other Stampeders at day's end, he could easily have fallen asleep over his food if it weren't for the excruciating cramps in his legs.

Jack took heavier and heavier loads. But even at one hundred pounds a load, to tote eight hundred pounds only two miles required hiking a total of thirty miles, there and back. Sometime after eleven trips, he had only managed to move his and Shepard's outfits a mere mile.

On the trail, Jack had a lot of time to run numbers over and over in his head. He figured that in order to cover the entire Chilkoot, it would require a man to walk a total of five hundred miles, and half of that uphill.

In spite of this gargantuan task, Jack grew confident, cocky, as he got stronger. He even challenged some of the native porters, claiming he could now carry one hundred and fifty pounds of gear at a time. And he did it, too.

But where did young Jack get all that confidence?

When he was fifteen, he had borrowed three hundred dollars to buy a small sloop called the *Razzle-Dazzle*. He loved the freedom of sailing in San Francisco Bay, and he dreamed of adventures crossing oceans, anything to escape the life of the "work beast," holding down all those menial jobs to earn enough to help his family survive.

With his new boat, and inspired by some tough Oakland wharf companions, he decided to become an oyster pirate and raid the commercial oyster beds for profit. It was dangerous work done under the cover of night. Armed guards patrolled the oyster beds—getting caught would mean prison time. To dash in and out with the oysters, Jack had to use all his sailing skills. He loved the work and thrilled at the challenge.

When other boys his age were studying for college, Jack lived a restless, nomadic life. He spent less time reading books and made more money in a week selling stolen oysters than he ever could earn in a year of working in a factory.

None of the "pirates" was more daring and successful than

Jack London. Soon his cronies called him the "Prince of the Oyster Pirates." Jack's confidence in himself grew. A regular at a bar on the Oakland waterfront called the First and Last Chance Saloon, Jack hung about with seamen. He was a good fighter, an excellent sailor, and a famous drinker.

About this time, even Jack started to worry about his drinking habits. Still only in his late teens, he knew his days might be numbered if he kept drinking so much in the saloons. One day, staggering drunk, he plunged into the bay and nearly drowned as the riptide tugged him toward the open sea. After four hours floating in the icy water, he was plucked out by a Greek fisherman.

Jack decided he must control his drinking. He wanted bigger things for himself. He wanted to explore the world beyond Oakland—he craved romance and adventure.

Having never tried deep-sea sailing, Jack trained himself to sail small boats in all kinds of weather and began to hang out with deep-sea sailors from the sealing fleet wintering in the bay. He soon signed on as boat-puller for the next cruise of the three-masted schooner *Sophia Sutherland*, heading to the coast of Japan and the Bering Sea to hunt seals.

Now, four years after that deep-sea experience, Jack's wild spirit and hunger for adventure drove him up the fabled Chilkoot Trail. For days, Captain Shepard tried bravely to keep up with the younger men as the climb steepened, but every joint ached from arthritis. Finally, on one of the hottest days so far, the sixty-year-old confessed he couldn't continue another step. He was in too much pain and knew he'd only hinder Jack and the others. So he decided to turn back. Inside, he felt crushed. All the money and effort it took to get to the Klondike suddenly seemed wasted. He hugged Jack and shook hands with the others, and walked slowly down the trail from where they'd come.

Sloper, Thompson, and Goodman were deeply relieved when Shepard chose to go back to California. Someone said under his breath, "Finally," as Jack watched his brother-in-law disappear down the trail, a great relief for him, too.

They all turned, put the next loads of gear on their backs, and slogged up the endless trail toward Sheep Camp, the site of a large encampment of Stampeders who were organizing and resting before the final push over the summit.

Resting on the trail
(Museum of History & Industry, Seattle, shs16668)

DEAD HORSES

THE NARROW TRAIL in the hot August rain was choked with horses and mules panting and pulling freight through muck and drizzle as the climb grew even steeper. Stampeders pitched their tents haphazardly along the trail, everyone and everything the color of mud.

In the silence of concentrated hard work, Jack passed group after group of ragtag miners. Like Jack, none had bathed in weeks. Back then, no one took showers and baths the way we do today. Maybe in a hotel, maybe onboard a steamer, but certainly not on a trail. And everyone got used to the pungent smell of their companions.

With so many people passing over the same trail, it also became harder and harder to find uncontaminated water. Some people used toilet paper and buried their waste. There were outhouses at some of the bigger camps, but the usual way of going to the bathroom meant finding some bush or tree just off the trail and using leaves or water from a stream or snow to clean themselves.

Although some Stampeders carried guns on their belts, Jack didn't feel any sense of danger as he hiked. Everyone on the Chilkoot was driven by one goal alone—to get to Dawson before freeze-up and start mining for the yellow metal.

The horses paid the biggest price as they approached Sheep Camp. Their legs were cut and bruised from the rocks, and they'd grown as thin as snakes, starving as they climbed higher, where the vegetation faded away.

At night when Jack camped, he cooked pork and beans, baked bread in a frying pan, washed the dishes, then cut shavings and kindling for a breakfast fire before falling dead asleep in his bedroll, listening to the constant chatter of Thompson. Sometimes during dinner Sloper sharpened his knife, Jack his ax. One of them might mend pack straps, preparing for another day of agonizing work ahead. Big Jim Goodman, after roaming the hills with his gun, knocked out his pipe and pulled off his shoes for bed.

When Jack had a little energy at the end of the day, he'd strike up a conversation with a fellow countryman or a few foreigners who had come from as far away as Norway and Germany to strike it rich. He was very social, and he loved to share camp stories with strangers.

Jack would ask a ton of questions to everyone he met. He genuinely liked people, from hobos to sailors. Here, too, he enjoyed

listening to the tales told by Stampeders, even when they were tall tales told by veteran miners returning from the Klondike who tried to scare the newcomers.

One night, a man camping nearby, who was just back from Dawson, talked over the fire about Bonanza Creek, where men were finding gold everywhere. The prospector had nuggets in his pockets the size of walnuts. He said, "You can just reach into the stream and grab these things." He pulled out a nugget and rolled it around the palm of his dirty hand. The light from Jack's fire twinkled off the shiny gold material like a dream come true.

This gold, the old miner said, was everywhere in those streams, and deep in the earth, too. Stories like his fed Jack's fever for gold and kept him from sleeping that night, even though he was plumb exhausted.

Next day, Jack and his partners found new energy to lug their outfits over the trail again. Especially garrulous Thompson. But tensions were running high even among friends. The stress of the trek pushed many to their breaking points. Miners began to curse each other. Sloper and Goodman got into it, but Jack kept them from fighting. They squabbled over who should cook and who should carry that day. Thompson said he'd much rather carry a pack and that most of the cooking had fallen to him, which made him very grumpy.

They heard the story about two men along the trail who got into a terrible fight and decided to go their separate ways. They had divided their gear in a ridiculous fashion. First, they cut their one and only tent into equal halves; then one of them took the stock of their only rifle while the other took the barrel. Each of them was sure he'd outwitted the other. Under the strain of the trail, some cheechakos had already started to go mad.

Yet in spite of the tensions, Jack felt a great sense of unity among his partners and among the Stampeders as a whole. What bound them like brothers was the hard work and the general fear of the last leg of the upward climb; everyone chatted constantly about the infamous Chilkoot summit ahead.

After Shepard left, Jack took on a new partner, a feisty sixty-six-year-old veteran prospector from Santa Rosa, California, named Martin Tarwater. He traveled light and didn't add to the group's gear. And he said he was good at repairing shoes and boots.

Tarwater made his case to be brought into the group: "I got a proposition, boys. You can take it or leave it, but just listen kindly to it. You're in a hurry to get in before freeze-up. Half the time is wasted over the cooking by one of you that he might be puttin' in packin' an outfit. If I do the cookin' for you, you all'll be better, and that'll make you pack better. And I can pack quite a bit myself in between times, quite a bit, yes, quite a bit." They looked at the wiry old buzzard and figured he wasn't lying, so they voted him in.

Tarwater's cooking skills were complemented by his energy for cleaning and hunting for dry wood. He freed up the other four to conduct the endless task of packing their gear up the trail. Thompson couldn't have been happier.

Jack's constant back-and-forth, miles and miles, only to move all his gear forward by a mere mile or two, felt like being in prison; at this rate he'd never make it to Dawson before winter. There was no escape from the toil. Yet he sweated and struggled

Pack trains on the Chilkoot Trail, which has been blocked by a fallen horse, 1897
(University of Washington Libraries, Special Collections, La Roche 2030)

on, every muscle and tendon inflamed when he crawled into his bedroll for a few hours of sleep. The campfires had turned his clothes to smoke rags, and he could fall asleep instantly no matter how much Thompson would chatter on.

As Jack moved closer to Sheep Camp, he smelled an even more pungent odor than the unwashed men—the rotting flesh of dead horses. He was again appalled by the way many treated their animals, as his writing about the White Pass (also known as the Dead Horse Trail) shows:

From Skaguay to Bennett they rotted in heaps. They died at the Rocks, they were poisoned at the Summit, and they starved at the Lakes; they fell off the trail, what there was of it, and they went through it; in the river they drowned under their loads, or were smashed to pieces against the boulders; they snapped their legs in the crevices and broke their backs falling backwards with their packs; in the sloughs they sank from sight or smothered in the slime, and they were disembowelled . . . men shot them, worked them to death, and when they were gone, went back to the beach and bought more. Some did not bother to shoot them— stripping the saddles off and the shoes and leaving them where they fell. Their hearts turned to stone—those which did not break—and they became beasts, the men on the Dead Horse Trail.

Some Chilkoot outfitters turned their horses loose when the trail got too steep for the weak ones to climb farther. Without anything to eat, the pitiful beasts hobbled through camp, tumbling over the guy wires of tents and rummaging through empty boxes for food. It broke Jack's heart to see them. So many horses starved near Sheep Camp.

SHEEP CAMP

THREE MILES FROM the summit, Sheep Camp was the last place for firewood and tent poles. The gorge they had followed for days opened into a broad valley. Jack's eyes panned across the chaos of tents and piles of goods sprawled over the open notch in the mountain. The swift river, maybe sixteen feet wide, poured through camp. Here were crowded saloon tents and a twenty-by-forty-foot wood structure with a sign out front that said HOTEL. It was one large room where scores of men flopped on the floor like dead fish to sleep at night.

Jack heard the crack of a rifle and saw a man putting his horse out of its misery rather than letting it die slowly of starvation. One man sat crying softly beside the trail that led into the camp. He'd lost all his gear over a cliff. Some had turned tents into stores and were trying to sell their supplies before heading home.

On a trail where hard-working men learned for the first time what work was . . . Driven desperately on by the near-thrust of winter, and lured madly on by the dream of gold, they worked to their last ounce of strength and fell by the way. Others, when failure made certain, blew out their brains. Some went mad, and still others, under the irk of the man-destroying strain, broke partnerships and dissolved life-time friendships with fellows just as good as themselves and just as strained and mad.

At Sheep Camp, Sloper, Goodman, Tarwater, Thompson, and Jack stood among bearded men for a photograph. The picture shows just how young Jack was on his Klondike adventure; he was by far the shortest and youngest-looking of the shabby Stampeders. He had a sensitive face and the eyes of a dreamer, yet those were also the fierce eyes of a man who would find his gold somehow.

In this photo at Sheep Camp from August 1897, Jack London is believed to be the shortest and youngest-looking man (see detail, second man from left).
(University of Washington Libraries, Special Collections, La Roche 2033)

The hardier Stampeders plodded on like oxen. Jack confronted the challenge of the Chilkoot head-on, just as he had done in every pursuit in his life. As he gladly left Sheep Camp, he skirted huge boulders blocking the trail and recalled the long, tedious hours shoveling coal to make money for his family back home. The memory injected new vigor into his movements. He threw another big load onto his back and trudged a short distance before dropping the pack and returning for more.

On August 23, in the rain and mud, three weeks after leaving Dyea, Jack and his partners camped in a less crowded spot above Sheep Camp. Tarwater whistled as he mended everyone's shoes.

Some days were warm and rainy; others were raw cold and rainy, though at any moment the shifting weather could blow snow and ice. Blizzard conditions were common. And now that they had climbed above the tree line, nighttime temperatures dipped well below freezing. Occasionally, if he could build a fire with wood carried from below, Tarwater managed to cook mush, fried bacon, hot rolls, and coffee for breakfast. Stiff and sleepless, the others woke to the old man's good cheer and constant humming. Most days, breakfast was scant for lack of fuel, but Jack approached the snowline with a light heart.

A FEW WEEKS LATER, the Dyea River would swell into a wall of water that flooded Sheep Camp, picking up miners' outfits like toys and dashing supplies helter-skelter down the valley. This was caused by the collapse of a glacier dam that sent tons of water, rocks, and other debris down the steep mountainside and into the valley above the camp. At least one man died. Many Stampeders would take this as another sign to pack it in and return home.

In the three miles between Sheep Camp and the Scales (where gear was weighed before being taken over the summit into Canada), Jack, Tarwater, Goodman, Sloper, and Thompson climbed past another part of the trail, where, the following April, an avalanche would kill seventy miners in one of the worst disasters of the Stampede.

Native packers wisely refused to work in heavy, deep springtime snow, which the warm southern winds could make unstable. They knew the dangers of attempting to climb the Chilkoot in these conditions. But on April 3, 1898, a group of miners from the flat states of the Midwest were camping at the Scales when an avalanche hit them in the early morning. Some retreated downslope to Sheep Camp, only to be hit by at least two more blasts of snow, back-to-back. A massive wall of white death crashed down the slope, burying scores of men under fifty feet of snow.

Volunteers search for bodies after the Chilkoot avalanche of April 3, 1898.
(University of Washington Libraries, Special Collections, Hegg 202)

After a short, eerie silence, gunshots rang through the valley. Fifteen hundred Stampeders stopped their treks in order to help save people from the avalanche. As the victims lay buried in snow, rescuers hurried to dig them out, hoping to find some still alive. Legend says one woman looked feverishly for her man and found him lying with the dead. She refused to believe he'd departed. She threw herself on her lover, rubbed his chest for hours, and breathed air into his lungs, until, in a miracle of love, he opened his eyes and called her name. She was known as the Lady of the Chilkoot. (A variant of this story is that her "lover" didn't recognize her and had no idea who she was!)

Many of the dead from the avalanche were carried back to Dyea and buried in a small graveyard. Some of the bodies were shipped on steamers home to family.

TARWATER

WHEN JACK AND HIS PARTNERS replaced Shepard with Tarwater, they had no idea what a wonderful asset the old man would be. But he soon proved indispensable. Jack captured this remarkable character in his writing:

> Tarwater became a striking figure on a trail unusually replete with striking figures. With thousands of men, each back-tripping half a

ton of outfit, retracing every mile of the trail twenty times, all came to know him and to hail him as "Father Christmas." And, as he worked, ever he raised his chant with his age-falsetto voice. None of the . . . men he had joined could complain about his work. True, his joints were stiff. . . . He moved slowly, and seemed to creak and crackle when he moved; but he kept on moving. Last into the blankets at night, he was first out in the morning . . . and, between breakfast and dinner and between dinner and supper, he always managed to back-trip for several packs himself. Sixty pounds was the limit of his burden, however. He could manage seventy-five, but he could not keep it up. Once, he tried ninety, but collapsed on the trail and was seriously shaky for a couple of days afterward. . . .

Work! Old Tarwater could shame them all, despite his creaking and crackling and the nasty hacking cough he had developed. Early and late, on trail or in camp beside the trail, he was ever in evidence, ever busy at something, ever responsive to the hail of "Father Christmas." Weary back-trippers would rest their packs on a log or rock alongside of where he rested his, and would say: "Sing us that song of yourn, dad, about Forty-Nine." And, when he had wheezingly complied, they would arise under their loads, remark that it was real heartening, and hit the forward trail again.

One late afternoon when the men rested beneath a boulder, with Tarwater already up ahead making dinner, Big Jim Goodman said as he smoked his pipe, "Tarwater sure earned his passage with us, didn't he?"

Sloper agreed and said he should become a full partner.

Thompson quickly said, "NO way. The deal is that when we reach Dawson, he's on his own."

Jack listened but kept quiet. He was thinking how glad he was to have this ever-upbeat and feisty old man along instead of his arthritic and complaining brother-in-law.

THE SCALES

ON AUGUST 27, JACK finally lugged his outfit above three thousand feet, where the shrubs of the subalpine zone, caressed by swirling clouds, looked more like animal apparitions to the minds of exhausted men. No trees or shelter, only the stacks and stacks of provisions the miners would carry in hundreds of loads on the last terrible leg up and over the summit.

The Scales was indeed a pitiful place, full of crazed men in a cul-de-sac at the foot of a rock wall. Yet in all that gray, Jack noticed the unexpected dots of color where men had thrown bright blankets on the boulders to dry.

The scene above the Scales sent terror through Stampeder blood. It was a sheer wall of mountain with a tiny, thin line of humans leading straight upward. On August 28, 1897, Jack and his partners finally joined that long string of Stampeders pushing for the top. Everywhere along the trail could be spotted discarded gear: bits of worn-out boots and tin cans, and even crates and bags of flour, left there by men who had panicked at the sight of that last push to the summit.

These photos give an idea of what the majority of Stampeders went through as they left the Scales and headed up the last steep climb to the summit. Although Jack faced bad weather at the top, since he arrived here in late August, he would have seen less snow and a lot more rock.
(Library of Congress LC-USZ62-41760 & LCUSZ62-41761)

Out of the corners of his eyes, Jack saw remnants of glaciers. At times, he had to crawl on hands and knees from boulder to boulder, where stubborn mosses and hardy lichens thrived. An occasional alpine flower grew out of a crag near the site where Jack and his partners set up camp. When it got too dark to climb, the group dropped their blankets on the cold, stony ground and fell into dead-man sleep. Icy water ran everywhere in the rocks below their blankets. The wind howled like the voices of ghouls.

In the morning, Jack dragged his body off the hostile rocks to climb back up to the summit with another hundred-pound load. Hand over hand, pulling to the summit, Jack clenched and unclenched his fingers to keep them from cramping. He blew warm air through his fists.

Up that relentless face of broken rock fragments, he clawed his way out of the last of the dwarfed shrubs below and joined once more the twisting line of men, a long string of leaf-cutter ants marching up and over the crest, where they seemed to vanish.

Suddenly, Jack had to shake his head in disbelief. Someone near him was carrying a sled dog over his shoulders up the trail to the summit! It was just one of many crazy ideas of the Stampeders. Others brought large iron stoves. Someone said that the grand piano at the Palace Grand Theatre in Dawson had also been carried over the pass.

In another few months, unfazed by winter, the Stampeders would still be clawing and inching their way over the ice. On this final ascent, enterprising Stampeders would chop 1,500 crude stairs into the hard-packed snow for easier climbing, then charge a fee to use what came to be known as the Golden Stairs.

If you left the line leading to the summit, you were out of luck.
(University of Washington Libraries, Special Collections, Hegg 97)

Jack's problems in August were mud and constant cold rain. His boots sloshed heavily with something like liquid ice.

In that desperate line of men scrambling up the last five hundred feet of elevation, while his own load cut deep into his flesh, Jack saw some lose their toeholds and move to the side of the trail. In a few weeks, when it would be covered in snow, men would slide all the way back down and have to join the line again—if someone was kind enough to let them in.

After countless trips back and forth, battered and utterly out of breath, Jack finally reached the summit one last time. He

dropped his load and stepped out of the snaking line of ever-moving men.

He stood motionless at the top. He turned and looked down at the laboring miners gasping for air, lugging their stoves and crates and sleds and tents and beans and rice and beer and whiskey and boards and sometimes even their animals up the ridiculously steep face.

For a moment, Jack felt part of something bigger than just greed for gold. He lifted his eyes from the trail below him and gazed out through the gloomy mist that had settled over the coastal mountain chain.

He'd left California on July 25, and it was now the last day of August. He'd been on the journey for a month, and he knew he had perhaps two months more travel to reach Dawson (he figured he'd be lucky to get there sometime in October). He felt good that he'd made it this far, all the way to the summit, when so many had turned back. He had hauled thousands of pounds of gear in small but heavier and heavier loads. He'd grown stronger than he'd ever been in his life, even more than in the days when he'd shoveled coal for ten hours at a stretch to help support his family.

He was only twenty-one. The gold was waiting. The adventure stretched out before him. But something deeply troubled him.

He looked down at the rocky and shrubby land enshrouded in mist, and had time to think of his father—not John London, the man he had always thought was his father—but another man with whom he had exchanged letters just before leaving California.

In fact, it was only the month before Jack headed north that he learned the truth about his real father.

———— ◆ ————

FOR A BRIEF TIME, Jack's mom had lived with a man named William Henry Chaney, a cranky but avid astrologer, distinguished orator and lecturer, a traveling lawyer, editor, and preacher. In many ways, Jack was a lot like him—highly intelligent. Both of Jack's parents were eccentric freethinkers. They were similar to each other in many ways, but they could not get along. So by the time Jack was born John Griffith Chaney on January 12, 1876, in San Francisco, his father, William Henry Chaney, had already jumped ship.

Jack had a complicated and emotional mother. Flora Wellman was prone to depression and rages. She made money as a seamstress and piano teacher; she was always scheming to get rich. She also believed in spirits and conducted séances in their home (Jack was embarrassed by this when his classmates came over to the house).

Eight months after Jack was born, an older man named John London, who was living in Flora's rooming house, married Flora and gave her son his surname. John London was a carpenter and small-time farmer, and also a Civil War veteran who needed a wife to help raise his two daughters by a previous marriage.

He was a kind and gentle man, a stable influence in the family, and a good farmer. Jack had done thousands of chores on John London's small farms. Scraping for cash, John tried his hand at carpentry and selling sewing machines door-to-door, but he did best growing potatoes, corn, grapes, fruit, and olives. He raised chickens and kept bees.

Jack loved the man. Mostly he liked to listen to John London's adventure tales from his younger days, when he worked as a scout and Indian fighter, or so he said. John, in turn, had great faith in Jack. When Jack was madly preparing to depart for the Klondike, his parents weren't at all opposed to the upcoming adventure. John London thrilled to the idea. If he weren't seventy years old, he said, and prone to sickness (weak lungs and broken ribs), he, too, would go to the Klondike with Jack. Maybe even get healthy in that clean, crisp Yukon air! And he fully believed Jack would come home from the gold fields triumphant. "He'll come out all right, you watch his smoke, and come out big, mark my words. . . . Jack is going to make a success out of the Klondike— whether he digs it out of the grassroots or not."

Jack hated to leave John London behind, fearing—correctly— that he might never see him again. John died while Jack was in the Klondike.

THE WIND WAS STRENGTHENING at the summit. Jack felt winter closing in. Flakes of snow stung his face. An icy fog rolled down out of the gray sky with a brutal rain that kept alternating with snow.

Jack leaned over to pick up another hundred-and-fifty-pound load. He drew the strap around his forehead, adjusted the pack over the center of his spine, and turned toward the lakes, the river, and the gold in the creeks that was waiting for him.

DOWN TO LINDEMAN

NEARLY A MONTH into his hike, Jack's clothes hung on his thin frame like laundry on a stick. He'd had to tighten his belt a few times. Even so, he had become one of the strongest non-native packers over the 33-mile Chilkoot from Dyea to Lake Bennett. Although his partners had had money to hire packers to help them with that last haul to the summit, Jack had grunted his way up and over with his own gear.

He now walked on the muddy, tea-colored trail under hanging glaciers. In camp at night, he looked into the open sky above the mountains, where the iridescent reds and greens of the northern lights, the aurora borealis, swirled above him. He felt bewitched by so much silent movement of color and light, by the mute but spectacular fireworks in the night sky.

Today's hikers along the Chilkoot Trail find objects the Stampeders left behind more than a century ago.
(Photo: Peter Lourie)

Boots wore out in days and were cast away.
(Photo: Peter Lourie)

The next day, he and his partners passed hundreds of empty tins of canned food, evaporated milk, and beans, as well as broken beer bottles and discarded scraps of metal. He saw bits of new rubber boots already worn out by Stampeders toiling over such rocky ground.

Big Jim Goodman, Merritt Sloper, Fred Thompson, Tarwater, and Jack finally reached a place called Happy Camp, happy because the Stampeders were on the downhill slope past a series of pristine alpine lakes with names such as Crater Lake, Long Lake, and Deep Lake. Happy, too, because after the barren summit of the pass, the Stampeders were coming again to the tree line, where they would more easily be able to build fires to warm themselves (one Stampeder mentioned it cost him $5 for the wood to build a fire above the tree line: Since $1 then is worth about $28 now, that's $140 in today's money).

The clouds lifted off the glacier above, and the sun blasted down on the men. The frigid lakes mirrored the blue sky and ice-clad peaks. Jack could smell the coffee brewing over hundreds of campfires, and his spirits soared.

Deep Lake, one of the Alpine lakes just past the summit of the Chilkoot
(Photo: Peter Lourie)

In the morning after a night rain, Jack and his partners squeezed the water out of their itchy wool clothes only to put them back on. They passed through increasingly wooded country. "Scarcely could it be called timber, for it was a dwarf rock-spruce that never raised its loftiest branches higher than a foot above the moss, and that twisted and groveled like a pig-vegetable."

JACK HAD PLENTY OF TIME during the journey to roll over in his mind all he'd accomplished. In twenty-one years, he'd worked more jobs and had traveled and seen more of the world than many experience in a lifetime. But one of his happiest memories was of meeting a librarian who had changed his life when he was only ten years old. In the Oakland Public Library, Ina Coolbrith, a poet and magazine editor, noticed the young lad sitting there for hours until his eyes burned. One day she suggested a few books he might like, and from then on, Ina became Jack's literary coach, making lists of books that he consumed at two per week.

Jack's reading expanded to all kinds of subjects. He found escape and romance in literature, and he was able to roam the world in fiction and nonfiction. He read morning, noon, and night, even though he had chores at home and needed to work long hours at hard jobs. He took out library cards in every family member's name so he could check out more books. His best friend, Frank Atherton, called him an extremist, because whatever Jack London set out to do, he did it to the limit. When he played games and competed with other kids in school, he had to be a winner. Reading was no different. He was driven to excel. Winning was always Jack London's goal; he wanted to be the best reader ever.

———— • ————

AT HAPPY CAMP, the sun disappeared quickly. Occasional snow flurries and driving cold rain slowed Jack as he moved all his gear downhill. A man just back from Lake Lindeman told Jack and his partners there were no more trees left and all boat building had stopped. *Liars,* Jack thought as he quickly loaded three fifty-pound sacks of rice on his back and picked up his pace. From Happy Camp down to Lindeman, it was a man-killing race against winter. Jack later said, "Men broke their hearts and backs and wept beside the trail in sheer exhaustion. But winter never faltered. The fall gales blew." Snow flurries increased, and the last three miles to the lake took twenty-four miles of hiking, twelve of those under the weight of a full load.

On September 8, 1897, nearly paralyzed with exhaustion, Jack and his partners piled their outfits on the beach at Lake Lindeman. They made camp among a hundred and fifty tents of all shapes and sizes—army tents, pup tents, saloon tents.

Lindeman was a small tent city of mad boatbuilders.

After Tarwater's hearty meal of bacon and beans, Jack, Goodman, Thompson, Tarwater, and Sloper went to sleep instantly, beaten down but not taken out of the game just yet. The days were shortening fast. The wind shifted into the north

Lake Lindeman during the Gold Rush
(University of Washington Libraries, Special Collections, UW 26992)

and screamed off the lake, nearly ripping their tent from its stakes. Tarwater was jerking around in his bedroll, his legs running in his sleep. Goodman dreamed of hunting bear, and when Jack woke to stumble out into the night and pee, he remembered the typhoon in Japan and smiled.

PART TWO

SEPTEMBER 9–OCTOBER 9, 1897

DOWN THE YUKON RIVER
TO SPLIT-UP ISLAND

Stampeders build boats, possibly at Lake Bennett or Lake Lindeman, ca. 1898.
(University of Washington Libraries, Special Collections, UW 22172)

BUILDING AND LAUNCHING THE BOATS

JACK WOKE IN the morning to crisp, clean air sweeping off the long, turquoise-colored lake. He looked at the snow-frosted mountains above and smelled Tarwater's bacon frying. As he drank his coffee, he heard the rasp of many whipsaws cutting logs into crude boards to make boats.

Along with the metallic pounding of hammers on nails, some men were singing. Tarwater was humming his old tunes. The whole place looked like a crazy boatyard with sixty odd-shaped boats all being worked on at the same time.

Jack and his partners voted to join forces with three other men to build two boats near a stand of spruce five miles up a partly navigable creek that led into Lake Lindeman. Goodman, Sloper, and Jack began cutting trees while old Tarwater and Thompson finished packing the last of their goods down from Deep Lake. They also made daily ten-mile runs (five up and five back) to get food to the boat builders. At night around the fire, Jack told sea stories from his days sealing in the Bering Sea. Everyone played cards.

What made them nervous was the oft-repeated stories of a looming famine in Dawson. Jack later described the desperation in his story "Like Argus of Ancient Times":

> The last grub steamboats up from Bering Sea were stalled by low water at the beginning of the Yukon Flats hundreds of miles north of Dawson. . . . Flour in Dawson was up to two dollars a pound, but no one would sell. Bonanza and Eldorado Kings, with money to burn, were leaving for the Outside because they could buy no grub. Miners' Committees were confiscating all grub and putting the population on strict rations. A man who held out an ounce of grub was shot like a dog. A score had been so executed already.

Jack and his partners worked faster. But it was hard work sawing lumber with rusty and broken whipsaws in the cold and rain that would blot out the sun for days.

The patience of the men, often taken to its limit, could erode suddenly. Sloper blasted Thompson for not making the lines straight as they cut trees into logs, then sawed them into boards. The crude boards for the ships were ten inches wide and an inch thick. More or less.

Merritt Sloper was the master carpenter and boat builder whose advice everyone tried to follow. Jack drew lines on the top and bottom of a log, then placed it on a tall scaffolding, called a sawpit, to be whipsawed. Making boards the hard way, in what came to be known as a Klondike sawmill, one man would scramble on top and pull his end of the six-foot-long saw upward, so his partner on the bottom could pull down, making the cut; each thought he was doing all the work. The saw continually got jammed and stuck in the green lumber. It was impossible to keep the blade on the drawn line.

Goodman yelled down to Thompson, "Stop hanging on the saw when I'm trying to pull upward."

"I'm NOT," Thompson fired back at his angry partner, sawdust burning his eyes below.

Stampeders cut logs by hand at a "Klondike sawmill."
(University of Washington Libraries, Special Collections, Hegg 177b)

They traded places, and the bickering went on day after day,
truly hard work. Meanwhile someone called out, "Work together,
darn it. Find the rhythm!" Which really angered everyone.

Whipsawing could easily turn best friends into enemies. Jack
wondered if the partnership would hold during this time. But
the men worked fast and agreed to beat the onset of winter. First

the seams and cracks had to be sealed. For hours, Jack dipped stringy oakum into the boiling, sticky pitch, then forced it into the many seams, working it in carefully.

A week later, the boat was finished. Three more days went by, and on September 19, everyone struggled to work the boat with lines, down two miles of a swift and swollen river feeding into the lake. Then they all jumped aboard, letting it rip along the torrent with Jack at the stern, Sloper at the bow, and Goodman and Thompson at the oars. Now they were a team again.

After they went back to fetch the second boat, everyone ate a huge celebration supper, laughing and singing on the shore of Lindeman. Tarwater did a short jig.

Next day, Jack rigged the boom and the mast on both ships.

Stampeders embark at Lake Bennett.
(University of Washington Libraries, Special Collections, Hegg 229)

Goodman and Sloper sewed the sails until midnight. The men agreed to name their two twenty-seven-foot, flat-bottom boats the *Belle of the Yukon* and the *Yukon Belle*. They painted the names in large charcoal-black letters on the stern, and also on each side of the bow.

All the other Stampeders stopped building their own boats to help Jack and his crew set out for Dawson. Shouts of good wishes rose into the sky as the boats pushed into the lake. Revolver shots ripped the air.

On September 21, just under two months after he'd left San Francisco, Jack stood at the stern of one of the boats, sail catching the wind and driving it six miles an hour down the long lake, the mountains ahead white with snow to a thousand feet above the water.

The Stampeders built all kinds of crazy boats to travel the 550 miles to Dawson.
(University of Washington Libraries, Special Collections, Hegg 3052)

The beginning of their 550-mile water journey started with a series of lakes: first Lindeman, then Bennett, Tagish, and Marsh. In what seemed like no time at all, they jumped off the boats at the end of Lake Lindeman to portage their gear around a deadly, one-mile set of rapids separating Lake Lindeman from Lake Bennett. Jack again took charge of lining the boats through some deadly rocks. Now that Sloper had built them, Jack was in charge of the boats. He came to be known as Sailor Jack.

At Lake Bennett, more boats were being built. Above the beach, dead horses littered the hills. Many of these had come over the second trail from the coast, the White Pass, also called Dead Horse Trail, where so many horses and mules had starved or were shot that some said you could put all the dead animals together and walk the last miles of the trail on their carcasses without touching the earth.

MORE LAKES

JACK HATED SLEEP. He'd always hated sleep because it robbed him of living life to the fullest. He rose from his bed-roll before everyone else and prepared to leave the island on Lake Bennett where he and the others had camped the night.

They loaded the boats and shoved off. Both vessels were leaking terribly, the green wood shrinking and opening up the

same seams that had been caulked with oakum and pitch. All the gear and supplies that had been placed on slabs of wood above the bottom crossribs to keep everything dry were in danger of getting submerged. The men had to bail water constantly. It was sleepless and exhausting work.

The previous February, when Jack had been working at a steam laundry for fourteen hours a day, doing the work of two men, he had tried to write on a borrowed typewriter that had only capital letters. He needed five hours' sleep, he figured. So he set his alarm for six o'clock and counted back five hours, to one A.M. He'd permit himself to read and write until then. But most nights, he was so tired from laundry work, he fell asleep midsentence.

Jack now applied that same sleepless drive to the long river trip to Dawson. On September 23, a stiff wind took Jack and his two boats humming down Bennett in four-foot waves. The master skipper and all aboard had seen boats capsize when they tried to turn into the wind in their crude, homemade vessels. Those unfortunate Stampeders bailed for their lives as their craft teetered and then swamped. The men swam for shore while their gear went straight to the bottom of the cold, unforgiving lake.

Jack saw the skyline open into mountain ranges blanketed in vast forests and snowfields high above the water level. His gaze panned upward to where Dall sheep frolicked about the icy crags.

Camped on shore, in the morning they woke to snow and Tarwater's strong coffee and wry smile. Big Jim went out to look for moose but had no success.

MILES CANYON AND WHITEHORSE RAPIDS

AFTER THE LAST of the four big lakes, Jack's boat ran swiftly down the narrowing river until the water picked up speed through a hundred-yard-wide channel. He knew the river rounded a bend and then dashed in a loud roar through a box canyon only eighty feet wide. Its rock walls rose from fifty to one hundred feet high on both sides.

Jack heard the steady thunder long before he spotted the killer rapids of Miles Canyon. Pulling ashore in an eddy just above the white water, he and his partners got out to walk the canyon rim to study the torrent. They saw hundreds of fearful Stampeders taking their outfits out of their boats to drag all their gear around the canyon. Empty boats were then carefully guided down through the torrent with the use of lines. This would take an extra four days to accomplish.

The river squeezed through rock in a chaos of spume, waves, and wind. In the middle of it all was a spine of water eight feet high. Jack said, "We were in a hurry. Every one was in a hurry. . . . October was at hand, the land covered with snow, the river threatening to freeze up at any moment, and Dawson still hundreds of miles to the north." Confident mariner that he was, Jack voted to run the river here, something few Stampeders did. He wanted to drive his boat at twenty-five miles per hour through Miles Canyon in just a few minutes. Either he'd save a few days of hauling gear, or they'd die trying.

As was the custom whenever a big decision had to be made, they put it to a vote. Sloper said, "Let's do it!" Goodman, the same. Old Tarwater wasn't so sure until Thompson smiled and put his thumb up and said, "No time to pull everything around. I'm in!" It was unanimous.

Thompson and Goodman, untested in boats, took their positions side by side at the oars. Merritt Sloper went to the bow with a paddle; he'd told Jack he'd messed around in boats before.

Veteran sailor Jack stood in the stern holding the steering oar, called a sweep, which he lashed down so tightly to the boat it'd never give out.

"Keep on the ridge," the men cried from the canyon rim as Jack pushed off. The current instantly whipped them and their five thousand pounds of supplies into a watery storm that spun their skiff like a stick this way and that. On either side,

Running Miles Canyon
(Yukon Archives, Robert Coutts fonds, 78/69, #314)

the rock walls dashed by them "like twin lightning express trains."

Astonished Stampeders stared intently down at Jack's boat from high atop the canyon wall. Some wore smirks of "don't say I didn't warn you" as they watched the *Yukon Belle* fail to ride the main water ridge because of its immense weight. They watched it nose-dive its way along the trough of that ridge, plunging in and out of the chaotic water.

At the bow, Sloper paddled like a crazy man. Sometimes when the front of the boat kicked up high, he paddled so furiously he stroked pure air, like a windmill in a gale. The boat plunged through the air like a stone, and Sloper, hardly a hundred pounds, got buried in the crashing spume. But he always stood fast, emerging with his paddle in motion. He yelled some warning to Jack, but the sound of his voice was swallowed by the river thunder.

Jack motioned to Thompson and Goodman to put up their oars so they wouldn't catch the water and accidentally flip the boat. Meanwhile, Jack jammed the sweep oar with every ounce of his might to keep the boat from going sideways, which would mean instant death. He tried and tried to get the boat up on the ridge. Then he heard his oar crack, but luckily, it didn't break.

Sloper's paddle finally did break, but, suddenly, after one last header that gulped the entire boat, the river spat them out the other side of the canyon into a giant whirlpool. The heavy boat went totally limp.

Jack had done it, run a mile-long canyon in only three minutes, and they'd saved four days of time. The men on the rim cheered and threw their hats into the air.

After bailing the water out of the boat, Jack ran a few miles of "normal" rapids, passing wrecks on the rocks where lives had been lost. Then the group faced a much greater danger than Miles Canyon—the Whitehorse Rapids.

Also known as the Graveyard, these rapids had never successfully been run in previous years—everyone who had tried had drowned. Stampeders were portaging not just their supplies, but even their boats on skids of spruce logs placed side by side.

Apparently, the most dangerous part was the very end section, called the Mane of the Horse. A long reef of violent, foamy white water threw the whole river to the right bank, then abruptly

"jumped" back, rushing to the left into a giant and deadly whirlpool.

So when everyone heard that a guy named Jack London was attempting these rapids, hundreds and hundreds came to marvel. Surely, they thought, this would be the young man's undoing.

Jack was in a hurry and rather proud of his good luck, so not a pound was taken from the boat. The *Yukon Belle* leaped clear of the water, then buried itself in the troughs of the waves until Jack completely lost control of his boat. A crosscurrent pushed the stern sideways, broadside. Sloper snapped a second paddle in the raging water. Waterlogged, the *Yukon Belle* then careened toward the left bank of the river, and no matter how hard Jack pushed the sweep oar (it cracked again), he could not turn the nose of the boat downstream. Everything happened at lightning speed. They hit the Mane of the Horse and went sideways into the deadly whirlpool.

Jack realized he was actually trying to buck the whirlpool, pushing the sweep the wrong way and locking them down, so in a flash of understanding, he changed the direction of his oar, which once again made a loud cracking sound, but the vessel answered instantly, missing the rocks by a couple of inches. Sloper, in fact, had already leaped to the top of the rock, but tumbled back "like a man boarding a comet" as the boat jogged forward.

THAT NIGHT, THEY CAMPED at the foot of the rapids in what would become the city of Whitehorse, capital of the Yukon Territory. Jack's reputation spread for miles. He'd run his boat through Miles Canyon *and* Whitehorse Rapids, fully loaded, saving eight days of hard portaging labor. And what was even more incredible is that Jack went back to run their second boat, the *Belle of the Yukon*, through the same canyon and rapids.

Although it was 420 river miles to Dawson, they now had a slightly better chance of getting to the Klondike before freeze-up. Of course, it was still a frantic race against winter. On the night of September 25, the temperature dropped well below freezing. Winds and nasty weather lay ahead on Lake Laberge, one of the most dreaded parts of the river route to Dawson.

Jack pushed onward.

LAKE LABERGE

A FAMOUS SCOTTISH DOG MUSHER, Allan Alexander Allan, or Scotty for short, described the next part of Jack's journey as "a series of flats, mountains, hills, water, mud, quagmires and bogs from one end to the other." It wasn't just Sailor Jack's boat-handling abilities that would get them through this part; he was also good at camping and roughing it. At eighteen, Jack had learned how to live rugged when he spent nine months crossing the country as a hobo. When Jack had returned more confident from his successful sea voyage on the sealing schooner the *Sophia Sutherland*, he fell into the old routine of hard work and low wages, but soon grew restless again. So he set off to cross the United States on freight trains. During his hobo adventure, he witnessed terrible poverty throughout the land. He got thrown in prison for vagrancy in Buffalo, New York, then traveled to Baltimore, Maryland; Washington, DC; and New York City, where he was horrified by the abject conditions of so many people living in slums.

Back again in California, Jack reflected on the people he'd camped with on the tracks and the people in the city slums. This vision of a struggling America helped him see that he too was a member of the underclass, and that he might easily fall into the poverty pit if he didn't struggle against the tide of destitution.

So after his trip across America, he vowed to change his life. In January 1895, Jack hit the books hard. He'd dropped out of school in the eighth grade in order to earn money for his family, but he now enrolled in high school. He knew that only education could save him from a life of hard labor and toil.

———◆———

BELOW THE WHITEHORSE RAPIDS, Jack and his group were forced by knife-cutting snow, howling winds, and darkness to grope for a campsite in a cove on thirty-mile-long, three-mile-wide Lake Laberge. They found a few sticks of driftwood for a fire, but the winds blew against them and they were forced to camp for three days. Ice formed in sheltered pools along the shores. Time after time, they tried to go out into the lake but barely got back to shore without tipping over.

More boats tied up nearby. Jim Goodman went out to shoot a bear but got only a pheasant. This delay greatly troubled Jack. Unless they got beyond Laberge immediately, they were doomed to be stuck here, frozen in for six months to come.

Stampeders dreaded Lake Laberge for good reason. Famous for unpredictable weather, fog, and tumultuous waves that could whip up in an instant, the lake was surrounded by a land covered in snow. Walls of rock shot down into the water, making it hard to find camping sites. The occasional wave-pounded, rocky beaches, where the rim ice had already begun to form, made for unfriendly campsites.

Their sixth day on the lake, Jack pushed them onward. He yelled out, "This day we go through. We turn back for nothing!" Day after day, the *Yukon Belle* and sister boat the *Belle of the Yukon* had unsuccessfully fought the cresting seas, the spray turning to ice. So now they rowed for their lives and even set sails against the monster waves and fierce winter storm. They rowed as hard as they had ever rowed, hands feeling like ice, and when they finally got to the end of the lake, where the river started again, they looked back to see the water on the lake had frozen solid, locking down all river travel until late May the next year. They were the last Stampeders to make it through in 1897.

As the Yukon narrowed and picked up speed, Jack recalled how hard it had been for him to be a student after having learned to live outdoors.

WHEN JACK ENTERED Oakland High School in January 1895, he wore a wrinkled dark blue suit and wool shirt. He sat at his desk looking tough, arms sprawled out in front of him, gazing around the room with an expression of haughtiness. He didn't like high school, so he found a shortcut to university by studying for the entrance exams. After cramming two years' worth of studies into three months—sometimes working nineteen hours a day at the books—he was accepted to the University of California at Berkeley, where he began his short career as a college student.

College life was also not easy for Jack, partly because he was classmates with many of the wealthier members of the ruling class of California; he came from humbler beginnings. He was eager to take all the English courses the university offered. He had big plans. With his mop of curly hair and broad shoulders, he gave off the aura of a man who had done wild, adventurous things. He was known as a brawler. He boxed with other students, though many were afraid of him. He also began to speak in public on street corners about the ills of big business, and was even arrested for doing so without a license. At twenty he was developing a reputation for public speaking and often drew a crowd.

In February 1897, after only one semester, Jack had to withdraw from the university to help with family finances. He began to pour all his energy into his writing, hoping to make money from the stories that he crafted deep into the night. He sometimes wrote for fifteen hours straight, forgetting to eat. He wrote with confidence, expecting editors any moment to discover his genius. Instead, his manuscripts were rejected and returned to him. He could hardly pay for the stamps of his submissions.

It was at this time that he discovered John London was not his real father and that he might be illegitimate, a bastard. Deeply disturbed by this and depressed from all his failed writing attempts, he solved his problems by heading out on another adventure: He joined the Stampede to the Klondike. If he could just strike gold, he would help his family and never have to do hard labor again. He'd be able to write for the rest of his life.

TRIBUTARIES SPITTING ICE

ESCAPING THE FROZEN LAKE, Jack and his partners were suddenly swept into the Thirty Mile River, which shoots out of the lake like water through a hose. Jack sat back at his sweep-oar, letting the six-mile-an-hour current carry the *Yukon Belle* a few miles closer to Dawson and the Klondike gold fields. Whenever they slowed, the mush ice clutched at their hull.

What a relief it must have been to make camp that night, with Lake Laberge behind them. Jack found a good camping place in the cold dusk, but had to shovel a lot of snow away in order to pitch the tent. They'd lost sight of the *Belle of the Yukon*. Oh well, thought Jack, they'd meet up soon enough.

For days, Jack and his partners worked hard to weave through ice and dodge the many rocks that could suddenly end their trip. He and his Argonauts entered a raw and vast wilderness inhabited by only a few nomadic Native tribes, some close to starvation, some suffering from tuberculosis.

On October 3, the group started out early in a dense fog and bitter cold. They found their sister boat and proceeded in tandem. The Big Salmon River, a tributary feeding into the Yukon, was throwing out tons of slushy ice, but they were able to go forty-five miles the next day, so swift was the current. Passing Little Salmon River, which sloshed even more ice into the Yukon, they encountered a band of Native families with large rings in their noses and ears. They were trading fish, meat, and moccasins. Jack's group bought a rabbit for fifty cents.

The boats ran onto a sandbar. Everyone got out and pushed and pulled them back up the river. Thank God for the strength and size of Big Jim.

The next day, the group successfully faced a dangerous but short set of rapids called Five Finger Rapids, then passed on down to Fort Selkirk, a trading post of the Hudson's Bay Company since 1848. Jack let the men stop for a half hour to look over the many Native dwellings strung along the riverbank.

In the main trading post was a "small stock of fancy-colored calicoes, a few guns and ammunition, moccasins, and skins, but no provisions of any kind [no riverboat had been here in two years]." Jack looked through the register on the counter, where 4,844 other Stampeders had written their names and hometowns. The storekeeper said several thousand additional Stampeders had not stopped, making perhaps a total of six thousand who had set course for Dawson by that autumn. A year later, this number would swell to forty thousand.

As the boats set off downriver, the swift current was congested with so much ice that casual drifting was now impossible. Jack steered the boat around dangerous "sweepers," fallen trees with massive roots still attached to the riverbank and ready to entrap anyone unlucky enough to get too close. In dense fog, Jack navigated through tons of slush ice pouring out of the wide Pelly River.

SPLIT-UP ISLAND AT STEWART RIVER

ON OCTOBER 8, Jim Goodman traveled out of camp and shot a lynx. Setting out on the river again, they began moving at a clip of fifty to sixty miles a day!

Two and a half months after leaving San Francisco, and four days after leaving Selkirk, Goodman, Thompson, Sloper, and Jack (Tarwater was on the other boat) pulled the *Yukon Belle* ashore on a low-lying island just below the mouth of the Stewart River, seventy-five miles short of Dawson. Massive spruce trees, cottonwoods, willow, and alder covered the island. Although there were no snakes, raccoons, or possums, other game was abundant in this part of the Klondike—marten, lynx, fox, beaver, wolf, wolverine, ermine, muskrat, grizzly, coyote, moose, and caribou.

Of the multiple islands here, the one Jack and his partners chose to spend the winter on was called Upper Island or Split-Up Island because it was a place where prospecting parties often split up to go their separate ways. A few years before, it had been a busy place, with a big mining camp nearby called Stewart City. Three hundred thousand dollars' worth of gold had been mined here, and more than thirty abandoned cabins dotted the islands along the river.

Jack had met so many defeated miners retreating upriver from Dawson, he and his group decided not to drift into town just yet. The dire warnings that Dawson was due for a famine were in fact coming true, and they wanted to scout this area first. Whereas all the creeks around Dawson had been staked with claims, Henderson Creek, flowing into the Yukon only a few miles from the island, was ripe for staking.

Named after the veteran prospector Bob Henderson, the creek had few claims on it. Although Henderson himself had put in his "discovery claim" (the term used for the first claim on a creek) only months before, there was plenty of room for more claims. So much gold had been taken out of the general area in former years, Henderson sure seemed to Jack like a good bet.

He took over one of the empty cabins on Split-Up Island, a perfect staging ground for his mining headquarters, he thought. On October 10, he went across the river to talk to an old-timer to get some pointers about the kind of country they were in. Then the Stewart froze up solid, and on the eleventh, Jim Goodman, who was the only experienced miner, scouted up Henderson

(the swifter creeks were still flowing, even though some of the larger tributaries of the Yukon had frozen), and he came back with positive reports. His pan had found "good colors," which means the creek had gold in it. He brought along some grains of gold to prove it. This was exciting news. You could hear whooping around the cabins.

Bright and early, Jack and Jim and two other miners in the area set off for three days of prospecting along Henderson. Sloper and Thompson remained in camp baking bread and pies and sharpening their axes. Sloper built a sled for the oncoming winter.

Like all prospectors, Jack's first task was to locate an area of the stream that might be good for mining. He was particularly interested in a portion of the left, or north, fork of Henderson. Second, he'd literally mark or "claim" the land by erecting posts with placards on all four corners of the plot. Then he'd have to register his claim at the gold commissioner's office in Dawson before he could start digging. Once the claim was registered, it would be protected from other miners who might want to encroach on it.

Leaving their cabins on Split-Up Island, Jack, Big Jim, and their new buddies walked four miles along the Yukon to where the tiny Henderson flowed into the bigger river, then seven miles up the creek to where it forked. They panned as they traveled. When they got two miles up the left fork, Jack was thrilled to find gold flakes—colors layered his pan! Later he described the process in his novel *Burning Daylight*.

He . . . began to wash. Earth and gravel seemed to fill the pan. As he imparted to it a circular movement, the lighter, coarser particles washed out over the edge. At times he combed the surface with his fingers, raking out handfuls of gravel. The contents of the pan diminished. As it drew near to the bottom, for the purpose of fleeting and tentative examination, he gave the pan a sudden sloshing movement, emptying it of water. . . . Thus the yellow gold flashed up as the muddy water was flirted away. It was gold—gold-dust, coarse gold. . . .

In three days, Jack and his partners staked eight claims on Henderson's north fork. When they got back to their cabins, Jack was euphoric. Along with Thompson and two other local

prospectors, he hopped aboard the *Yukon Belle* for the two-day journey to Dawson, where they'd all file their claims and get news of the outside world. They could collect any mail sent to them from home, and they might even get a shower in a hotel.

The Yukon was still open for travel, but only for a few more days. For sure they'd be forced to wait in Dawson until the mighty river froze deep and solid.

PART THREE

OCTOBER 16–DECEMBER 2, 1897

DAWSON

Dawson Waterfront, 1898

(University of Washington Libraries, Special Collections, UW 26618)

THE CITY OF GOLD

JACK HEARD THE HUBBUB of Dawson before he floated
up to its ramshackle shanties, crude log cabins, and riverboats of all sizes and shapes that stretched for a half mile along a
flat piece of swampy ground on the eastern bank of the Yukon.
Gentle hills of shrub fir and birch rose behind the town, and the
cold fog that rolled off the river gave the place a bleak air.

Located where the Klondike River flows down the valley to
join the Yukon, Dawson was a sea of tents in October 1897. The
town had no radios, no telephones, no telegraph even. The mail
sometimes wasn't delivered for months on end. There were no
sewers, just mud and raw living. Gold dust was the town's main
currency.

At all hours, the sound of hammers rang out in the now-wintry
air. Saloons and cabins went up in a matter of days.

The population of the town was little more than four

thousand when Jack got there, but would soon swell to many times that. Dawson streets ran parallel with the river. Sixty feet back from the river's high-water mark, Main Street supported small earth-covered log dwellings and two-story log hotels, saloons, dance halls, and restaurants. All social life was concentrated in this two-block section along the riverfront. Here was the teeming hub of the place. Jack pitched his tent near the center of all the activity and remained in Dawson for six weeks as winter set its teeth upon the land.

To relieve his boredom, Jack went to the saloons for comradeship, noise, and laughter. There he found "the long bar and the array of bottles, the gambling games, the big stove, the weigher at the gold-scales, the musicians, the men and women."

In the saloons, Jack and the other miners drank, argued, hollered, whooped, danced, and gambled. He especially loved to talk—that is, when he wasn't intently listening to the stories of the old-timers, the prospectors who had been in the Yukon long before the cheechakos arrived, the ones who really knew this country and who had traveled throughout the land. They were the *sourdoughs*, who made their bread not with baking powder (they had no baking powder) but with sourdough, hence the name. Jack had great respect for these old-timers.

After George Carmack, Keish (Skookum Jim) and Káa Goox (Dawson Charlie) had made their first big gold discovery, or "strike," and triggered the Stampede, the veteran miners who got in early soon came to be called Eldorado Kings. They pulled hundreds of thousands of dollars' worth of gold out of their claims.

All around Dawson, the creeks were alive with activity—some

people finding gold and some newcomers vainly looking for claims to work. And of course everyone was on the verge of making the next major strike! The place was electric with expectation.

Some of the biggest money was made not in finding gold, but rather in selling food and goods to miners. Just after the Carmack strike of '96, a French Canadian trader named Joseph Ladue saw a golden opportunity. While prospectors raced to Bonanza and nearby creeks to stake their mining claims, Ladue laid a different kind of claim to this mile of swampy land across the Klondike

George Carmack, with folded hands, standing in doorway of Klondike Hotel. Dawson. 1898.

George Carmack, with folded hands, stands with a group in front of the Klondike Hotel, Dawson, 1898.
(Yukon Archives, James Albert Johnson fonds, 82/341, #20)

Dawson quickly grew overcrowded, and supplies became hard to get.
(University of Washington Libraries, Special Collections, Hegg 2277)

tributary along the Yukon. He staked out city lots, then applied for a town site patent on his claim, and it became the city of Dawson (named after Canadian geologist George Mercer Dawson, who explored the area in 1887). In a few years, some of those lots would be worth as much as twenty thousand dollars apiece (over half a million in today's money). When the gold rush died down, Dawson continued to serve as the Yukon Territory's capital from 1898 until 1952, after which the government moved to Whitehorse, 460 miles upriver.

Walking around town, Jack felt the deep-chilled autumn days, foggy and bleak. Yet sometimes, during an extended Arctic high, the air would clear and become breathlessly beautiful and dry. Jack felt happier than he'd ever been in his life, except of course when he was out on the water somewhere sailing a boat.

Before Jack left San Francisco, all the newspapers had been predicting that people would starve in Dawson as the winter of '97 closed in. Supplies had dwindled to oatmeal, cornmeal, evaporated milk, evaporated potato, butter in cans, and bacon. Steamboats with fresh goods from the Bering Sea two thousand miles downriver had halted on October 1 because of impenetrable river ice. Yukon authorities told anyone without outfits to leave the territory to help lessen the effects of starvation in the looming winter.

Men who stayed in the country without enough supplies had it particularly rough. Horses had to be shot for food. There was even a story (a tall tale?) about one man in a lonely cabin who had died of starvation. His leg had been cut off by his ravenous partners and was boiling on the stove when help arrived.

PRICES IN DAWSON: 1897–1898

(Multiply by 28 to get a sense of what these would cost today.)

Candles: $1
Yukon stoves: $40–$75
Dogs: up to $400
Horses: $3,400 per pair

Moccasins, moose-hide, Native-made: $7
    (formerly 50 cents per pair)
Mittens, Native moose-hide: $6–$10 per pair
Men's deerskin parkas: $50–$100
Firewood: $35–$75 per cord
Copy of Shakespeare's works: $50

WAGES IN DAWSON

Ordinary miners: $1–$1.50 an hour
Foremen in mines: $15 and upward per 10-hour day
Bartenders: $15 per day
Bookkeepers: $17.50 per day
Musicians: $17.50–$20 per day
Services of man and two-horse team: $10 per hour
Drivers: $300 per month, plus board
Cooks in restaurants: $100 per week, plus board
Waiters: $50 per week, plus board for men;
    $100 per month, plus board for women
Barbers: 65 percent of receipts of chair, $15–$40 per day

A photojournalist named Tappan Adney, who was covering the story of the Stampede for *Harper's Weekly*, came off the ice-choked river in October 1897 and described the town as nothing more than a few dwellings built on a swamp, an oozy muck in the summer, and hard, dry land in the winter. The north end of town terminated "in a narrow point at the base of a mountain conspicuous by reason of a light-gray patch of 'slide' upon its side bearing resemblance to a dressed moose-hide in shape and color, which has given to it the name of 'Moose-hide' or 'Moose-skin' Mountain."

Often referred to simply as the Slide, the mountain appeared, and still appears today, to have been cut away with a giant's shovel. One day around Thanksgiving, a dance-hall performer threw a lighted kerosene lamp at a rival who was trying to steal her man. The wood building went up in flames, as did many of Dawson's buildings.

When Jack London and Tappan Adney landed at Dawson, with its three hundred cabins and stores, a small police post supported only a few policemen. A year later, by October 1898, in addition to a growing number of Mounties, the Yukon Field Force (the Canadian army presence in the Yukon) would send a detachment of fifty men to Dawson to help maintain order among the Stampeders.

In November, the thermometer often dropped to –25°F. A few inches of snow lay on the ground and the roofs of the buildings. All kinds of restless newcomers were milling about the little bit of walkway along the storefronts. Cheechakos wore mackinaws and heavy cloth caps. Sourdoughs wore deerskin coats or parkas with lynx, sable, mink, or beaver caps and big fur-lined, moose-hide mittens.

Men mostly, but an occasional woman, hurried every which way, with and without packs on their backs. A woman might be wearing a squirrel-skin coat in the dropping temperature.

"Dogs," Adney wrote, "both native and 'outside,' lay about the street under every one's feet, sleeping—as if it was furthest from their minds that any one should hurt them—or else in strings of two to ten were dragging [on dog sleds] prodigious loads of boxes or sacks intended for the mines or for fuel, urged on by energetic dog-punchers."

Third Street, Dawson, Yukon Territory, ca. 1899
(University of Washington Libraries, Special Collections, Hegg 858)

And still thousands kept arriving. Many of them, including women and children, did not come with their own outfits. They had to buy food and equipment and would eventually deplete the town's limited supplies. Adney says, "Excited men gathered in groups on the streets and in the saloons, and with gloomy faces discussed the situation. Some proposed seizing the warehouses and dividing the food evenly among all in camp."

THE BOND BROTHERS AND THEIR CABIN

SOON AFTER ARRIVING in Dawson, in a hotel saloon, Jack met two mining engineers named Marshall and Louis Bond. The Bonds, also from California, had arrived in Dawson just before Jack. They'd bought a cabin on the north side of town near the new hospital. Yale-educated and wealthy, they were sons of a California judge and mining entrepreneur. Marshall and Louis Bond were good company for Jack. Like him, they were well-read. They liked to sit around talking about interesting subjects.

Marshall later described meeting Jack in the Dominion Bar looking as unkempt as a hobo:

> One of these men was of medium height with very square broad shoulders. His face was marked by a thick stubbly beard. A cap pulled down low on the forehead was the one touch necessary to complete the concealment of head and features, so that that part of the anatomy one looks to for an index of character was covered with beard and cap. He looked as tough and as uninviting to us as we doubtless looked to him.

The Bonds rented a space beside their cabin to Jack and his partners, who set up a modest tent, into which they fitted a small Yukon woodstove for heat and cooking. (The Yukon stove was one of the chief items in the gold rush. It was a lightweight portable stove consisting of a small metal box, sometimes half a metal barrel, divided into a firebox and an oven. It was easily taken apart and carried in pieces over the Chilkoot.)

In the tent, Jack put down spruce boughs under his bedroll. The Bonds let him store food on the roof of their cabin so the roaming dogs wouldn't get into it. Firewood was so expensive, Jack and others saved money by heading to the saloons to hang out for hours on end. But Jack also loved talking with the Bonds and their friends in their cabin near his tent. Marshall Bond said the effect of Jack's words was hypnotic.

Jack finally registered his claim on Henderson in the office of the gold commissioner on November 5, 1897. Jack's plot—"more particularly described as placer mining Claim No. 54 on the Left Fork ascending Henderson Creek"—was two and a half miles, and fifty-four claims, above the fork where Robert Henderson had staked his discovery claim.

To get a sense of how crowded the area got over the next year, consider this: In June of 1897, only eight hundred claims had been filed in Dawson. Seven months later, there were five thousand claims, and by September 1898, ten months after Jack filed his claim, there were a total of seventeen thousand registered claims.

St. Mary's Hospital. In the detail, you can see a cabin (with ladder) and with a "cache" side cabin, and tent pitched nearby. This may have been in the actual place where Jack pitched his tent.

(Jim Robb Collection, Yukon, Canada)

FORM H.

APPLICATION FOR GRANT FOR PLACER MINING,

AND AFFIDAVIT OF APPLICANT.

I, *Jack London Yukon Dist*
of *Dawson in the Yukon Dist*
hereby apply, under the Dominion Mining Regulations, for a grant of a claim for
placer mining as defined in the said Regulations, in *the Henderson Creek*
Mining Division of the Yukon Dist
More particularly described
as placer Mining Claim No.
54 on the Left Fork Ascending
Henderson Creek in the aforesaid
Mining Division

and I solemnly swear :—

1. That I have discovered therein a deposit of *Gold*

2. That I am, to the best of my knowledge and belief, the first discoverer of
the said deposit ; or

3. ~~That the said claim was previously granted to~~
~~but has remained~~
~~unworked by the said grantee for not less than~~

4. That I am unaware that the land is other than vacant Dominion Land.

4. That I did, on the *16th* day of *Oct* 189 *7*
mark out on the ground, in accordance in every particular with the provisions of
~~sub-section (e) of clause eighteen~~ of the ~~said~~ Mining Regulations, the claim for
which I make this application, and that in so doing I did not encroach on any
other claim or mining location previously laid out by any other person.

for the
Yukon Ros
& its Terr-
-itories

6. That the said claim contains as nearly as I could measure or estimate an
area of *260 000* square feet, and that the description ~~and sketch~~
of this date hereto attached, signed by me, ~~sets~~ forth ~~in~~ in detail, to the best of my
knowledge and ability, its position, form and dimensions.

7. That I make this application in good faith to acquire the claim for the sole
purpose of mining to be prosecuted by myself, or by myself and associates, or by
my assigns.

Sworn before me at *Dawson*
in *the Yukon Dist* *Jack London*
this *5th* day of *Nov.*
189 *7* *Thos Fawaltt*
Gold Commissioner

Form No. 110.

LINGERING IN DAWSON

JACK STAYED IN DAWSON for forty-seven days before returning to Split-Up Island. That autumn, the cold weather mixed with unusually mild temperatures until late November, when the temperature finally plummeted to −60°F. So the Yukon took longer than expected to freeze solid enough for safe river travel. All through October, the rim ice had been thickening, and the Yukon carried a run of mush ice. When the Yukon River first begins to freeze, it is impassable for six to seven weeks—the ice is too slushy and soft to travel on and too thick for a boat to pass through. All river travel comes to a halt.

November got very cold in Jack's meager tent. In *The Klondike Stampede*, Tappan Adney describes living in Dawson a few miles from Jack:

> During all this time we lived in the tent, which was strung by a rope between two trees. The thermometer fell to 39° below zero, but it was astonishing how warm a stove made the tent; as soon as the fire went down, however, it was as cold as out-of-doors. Between us we had thirteen pairs of blankets, thin and thick, and in the midst of these we slept; even then, with all our clothes on

(OPPOSITE PAGE) This is the actual form Jack filled out to file his claim in Dawson in November 1897.
(Yukon Archives, GOV 387, #2080)

and lying close together, we were never really warm; but in time we grew accustomed to what we could not avoid. A great annoyance was caused by the steam of our breath and from our bodies condensing and freezing, until the white frost about our heads looked like that around a bear's den in winter. The breakfast fire would quickly melt the frost; but we never dried out.

While Jack waited for the Yukon to freeze, he kept returning to the saloons, dance halls, and gambling joints, where he soaked up the stories and the sights and the sounds of the gold rush. Jack had a powerful memory, and these details would later come to life in his writing.

Soon to be called the Paris of the North, Dawson had six

Jack loved to listen to the sourdoughs in Dawson saloons.
(University of Washington Libraries, Special Collections, Hegg 3143)

thousand inhabitants that fall. By the time Jack left the Klondike the following summer, the population had grown to thirty thousand. President William McKinley had to organize relief for those starving in the Yukon.

An article appeared in the Spokane, Washington, *Daily Chronicle*:

RELIEF WILL BE SENT TO KLONDIKE

PRESIDENT McKINLEY WILL URGE IMMEDIATE ACTION FOR RELIEF.

All the Members Anxious to Send Aid to the Gold Seekers.

Washington, Nov. 30.—The cabinet today considered the subject of sending relief to the people of the Klondike. The president has received a telegram from the Portland, Oregon, chamber of commerce, stating there was danger of destitution and suffering in the Klondike and offering to supply the necessary food for relief if the government would undertake the transportation.... No attempt will be made to go up the Yukon, as the ice has closed progress in that direction. Relief supplies will have to be sent over the passes.

While some began to feel the deep pangs of hunger, Jack walked around town observing all the many characters who had gathered in this boom city.

BIG ALEC McDONALD, KING OF THE KLONDIKE

ONE NOTABLE PERSONALITY Jack is certain to have met in town was Big Alec McDonald.

All the cheechakos drooled at the success story of Big Alec. A common statement about the Stampede is that of the forty thousand who reached Dawson, only a few hundred got rich. The luckiest of all might have been Alexander McDonald, a lumbering, almost clumsy man from Nova Scotia, Canada. Big Moose, as they called him, was a shrewd businessman. He'd climbed over the Chilkoot in 1896 and settled in Dawson. One of the claims he bought was Claim 30 on Eldorado Creek. He paid a Russian immigrant a sack of flour and a side of bacon for a claim that would soon yield more gold than almost any claim in the gold rush.

Big Alec rarely mined his claims himself, but rather leased them out to miners who were promised a split of whatever they discovered. He used the profits from claim 30 to buy other claims. By the end of 1897, he owned twenty-eight claims on many different creeks. In 1898 some said he was worth ten million dollars. He kept a suite at his own hotel—the McDonald Hotel. Visitors dipped their hands into a box of gold nuggets. He told them to grab just the big ones!

Marshall Bond wrote:

There is scarcely what you would term a trained businessman in the country, one of ability and comprehension of the situation. The most prominent figure is Alexander McDonald, a laborer of Scotch extraction. He bought a claim on Eldorado last year . . . and made a lot of money. He is a terrific plunger and buys right and left, often borrowing money at ten percent a month. He owed $150,000 some time ago, and his creditors thought they had him. In one day he took $30,000 out of the ground and saved himself. It is hard to tell what he is worth, perhaps millions, perhaps nothing.

New York Herald reporter John D. McGillivray wrote about Alexander McDonald and the power of the few storeowners who had set up shop:

There is in Dawson no newspaper, no bank, no such thing as an insurance office, no shops except those of the two trading companies, where the clerks are to be bowed down to.

They are most insolent in their manner of charging 3,000 per cent profit for a candle. One in Dawson must consider that he is being done a great favor to be allowed to purchase anything, and it is a curious sight to see "Alex" McDonald, worth several millions, endeavoring to be very polite to a puny clerk from whom he wishes to buy a few pounds of nails for one of his hundred cabins.

Big Alec tended to rub his chin slowly when new propositions were pitched to him. He would often say "no, no, no," and then he'd say "all right" to the claims he thought worth pursuing. Truly he was the King of the Klondike, one of the so-called Eldorado Kings, but after touring Europe and marrying a young woman in England, he squandered his money and died penniless, alone in a cabin on a small creek. He had spent his fortune and had given away much of it to the church.

THE DOGS OF DAWSON

IN DAWSON, THE BOND BROTHERS had two dogs named Pat and Jack, which they'd acquired in Seattle on their way north. They noticed how London didn't fawn over the dogs but rather let them come to him. He was a dog person, and he was particularly fond of the one called Jack, a cross between a Saint Bernard and a German shepherd. He had character. He was confident and courageous and immensely strong. He was intelligent and had a good nature. But, Jack knew, like any animal who might be treated badly, there was always the possibility the wolf in him could surface if he was pushed too far. Later he would become the model for Buck in London's most famous novel, *The Call of the Wild*.

Getting mail in and out of Dawson by dog team after the snows fell and the rivers froze solid was essential to the workings of the Canadian government, and London paid particular

"BUCK" of THE CALL OF THE WILD.
Owned by the Bond Brothers.
Dawson,N.W.T.,May 21,1898.

*Marshall and Louis Bond's cabin in Dawson. The dog on the left
is Jack, the model for Buck in* The Call of the Wild.
(Special Collections and Archives, Middlebury College)

attention to the hard work of delivering the mail. Strong, good
dogs like Jack would be made leader of an official dog team working back and forth between Dawson and the coast, a round-trip
of more than a thousand miles that foiled many Stampeders.

The dogs traveled the route regularly. Twenty-five- to thirty-
day trips were considered a good time for a dog team from Dawson
out to Dyea in early winter; eighteen days to return in spring. The
fastest time was ten days.

Jack met a man named "Klondike" Mike Mahoney, who ran
dog teams hauling freight and mail from the Alaskan coast all
the way to Dawson and back. Jack asked Mike so many questions about his job that Mike later remembered that of the

seventy people in the Split-Up camp that Christmas, one young man with great curiosity had sat for hours picking his brain. Later, that information found its way into Jack's Klondike stories.

In fact, Dawson, where so many dogs ran around the waterfront streets, was the ideal setting for Jack to observe how the animals were cared for by some and mistreated by others. He also noticed that some were half-breeds. Wild wolves tended to be shy of humans. But many of the Dawson dogs were hybrids: part wolf, part dog. Jack watched the ravenous dogs in Dawson, more than fifteen hundred of them, roam in fierce gangs around town. Many more were used out in the mines on the creeks. They traveled in packs of up to twenty, and when they saw a single dog, they chased it. Dogfights broke out all over town.

Jack found plenty of organized dogfights in Dawson, too. One such scene found its way into his novel *White Fang*, where the hybrid "fighting wolf" by that name finally meets his match on the outskirts of town, far enough into the woods that the Mounties wouldn't find the illegal fight. In White Fang's deadly tangle with the bulldog Cherokee, White Fang, who has successfully beaten every dog until now, is not able to counterattack with his usual wolf snip and back pull. The smaller Cherokee gets White Fang by the throat and nearly strangles him to death while White Fang's new and evil owner, Beauty Smith, kicks White Fang to get him angry so he'll fight harder.

It began to look as though the battle were over. The backers of Cherokee waxed jubilant and offered ridiculous odds. White

Fang's backers were correspondingly depressed, and refused bets of ten to one and twenty to one, though one man was rash enough to close a wager of fifty to one. This man was Beauty Smith. He took a step into the ring and pointed his finger at White Fang. Then he began to laugh derisively and scornfully. This produced the desired effect. White Fang went wild with rage. He called up his reserves of strength and gained his feet. As he struggled around the ring, the fifty pounds of his foe ever dragging on his throat, his anger passed on into panic.

***

OUTSIDE OF TOWN, in the low cranberry bushes that would turn red the next August, Jack came across bear tracks twelve inches long and eight inches wide. Once, roaming the surrounding hills, he confronted a timber wolf, face-to-face. Jack didn't see the animal, spectral gray in the frozen half-light, until he was only thirty yards away. Yukon wolves are the largest in the world. This wolf stood firm and confident near Bonanza Creek. Man and beast stared at one another for what seemed to Jack like half a minute. Then, on its own quiet terms, the timber wolf, confidently, ever cautiously, stepped backward a few paces, its

yellow eyes still fixed on Jack. Slowly it turned its head to the creek and sauntered down into the gully.

Wolves are social and highly intelligent creatures. They embody the spirit of free and unspoiled wilderness. Jack's nickname would become "Wolf." And his collection of published stories, *The Son of the Wolf*, would be his first of many Klondike tales.

PART FOUR

HENDERSON AND THE CREEKS

I wanted the gold, and I sought it;
I scrabbled and mucked like a slave.
Was it famine or scurvy—I fought it;
I hurled my youth into a grave.
I wanted the gold, and I got it—
Came out with a fortune last fall,—
Yet somehow life's not what I thought it,
And somehow the gold isn't all.

No! There's the land. (Have you seen it?)
It's the cussedest land that I know,
From the big, dizzy mountains that screen it,
To the deep, deathlike valleys below.
Some say God was tired when He made it;
Some say it's a fine land to shun;
Maybe: but there's some as would trade it
For no land on earth—and I'm one.

From "The Spell of the Yukon,"
by Robert Service

HENDERSON CREEK

WITH HIS CLAIM LEGALLY FILED, Jack had to do some mining. Soon he'd begin the backbreaking work of digging a shaft into the frozen ground of his claim.

On December 3, the ice on the river was safe for travel. After so many weeks of muddy streets, saloons, and dance halls, Jack and Fred Thompson finally put Dawson behind them. Yet it felt a little lonely to leave the company of the Bond brothers and their educated friends and all the excitement of the town. Heading out to a cabin seventy-five miles away, Jack would face the long and bitter cold of the fast-approaching dark winter.

He left town on snowshoes. When he'd first tried snowshoeing, he grew exhausted at the end of a hundred yards. He learned quickly that walking in deep snow with snowshoes was hard work: "At every step the great webbed shoe sinks till the snow is level with the knee. Then up, straight up, the deviation of a fraction of an inch being a certain precursor of disaster, the snowshoe must be lifted till the surface is cleared; then forward, down, and the other foot is raised perpendicularly for the matter of half a yard."

They camped for four days on the river until they found their island silent and white. "No animals nor humming insects broke the silence. No birds flew in the chill air. . . . The world slept, and it was like the sleep of death." The river was covered now in three feet of ice with three feet of snow above that.

As the gloomy light of the shorter Arctic days dwindled to just a few hours, from his cabin Jack watched the men hiking from the Chilkoot to Dawson. They etched a thin dark line on the great white expanse. The Stewart camp just happened to be located at a kind of Stampeder crossroads, with miners constantly moving to and from Dawson. Jack liked meeting the prospectors as they traveled through.

At Split-Up, Jack met a miner named Emil Jensen. From the moment Emil landed his boat in the swift, icy current, the two men became best pals. They shared books and laughter through the cold winter. Emil remembered first meeting Jack, that "curly-haired, blue-eyed boy . . . little more than a lad," yet with a "face illumined with a smile that never grew cold."

Jack and his partners immediately talked up Henderson Creek. Emil wrote later, "Many others joined in our conversation, all singing the praises of Henderson. All were Henderson mad. Rich? Why, a shovel thrust into the creek-bed—where the swift water kept the ice at bay—had brought up a dollar's worth of shining dust in the bit of gravel clinging to its blade. . . . Was it

Fate, or was it the usual stampede madness—gold madness? Oh, of course we all fell for it."

Emil and his own partners decided to stay with Jack. They took up residence in an empty shack just behind Jack's cabin in order to explore Henderson Creek.

The owner of Claim 54, Jack now gathered his gear and made his way thirteen miles up Henderson Creek.

CABIN LIVING

FOUR MILES BEYOND his claim, Jack helped build a small cabin only twenty feet from Emil Jensen's shack, then both started the grueling work of mining in winter. Emil said later, "Like the others, he toiled, sweated and flung the dirt about with an enthusiasm that never diminished."

Although Jack wasn't keeping a journal at the time, he later wrote that a miner's cabin was no bigger than ten by twelve feet, snug and heated by a roaring Yukon stove. It felt "more home-like to him than any house he had ever lived in." A few bunks, a table, and the stove took up most of the room, "but every inch of space was utilized. Revolvers, rifles, hunting-knives, belts and clothes, hung from three of the walls in picturesque confusion; the remaining [wall] . . . being hidden by a set of shelves, which held all their cooking utensils."

Dick North and friends discovered Jack's cabin on Henderson in 1965 and salvaged its parts so replicas could be constructed in Dawson and California.
(Photo: Peter Lourie)

Life in a small cabin on an isolated creek was not easy. Tensions grew and tempers blazed. It was difficult to cook in a crowded little cabin. There was hardly enough space for three or four men to eat, sleep, lounge, smoke, play cards, and entertain visitors, and all their personal gear was stored anywhere they could find a spot. When you came in from the outside, you used the whisk broom hanging at the entrance to brush the snow off your clothes before you settled into cabin life.

The miners never made their beds—blankets on pine needles for a mattress or caribou skins placed on spruce-pole bunks—and their stuff was flung all over the place. The Yukon stove in one corner of the cabin radiated all the heat they needed, even in temperatures of −60°F outside. In the morning, the cook rose to rekindle the fire that had dwindled in the night, but he also had to go out and fetch water and wood. Tarwater was no longer part of the group, so everyone took turns cooking.

The cabin had a dirt floor. They did a lot of carpentry work inside, and the chips and shavings were never swept up because they helped insulate against the cold. Jack jokingly wrote, "Whenever he [the cook] kindles a fire he uses a couple of handfuls of the floor. However, when the deposit becomes so deep that his head is knocking against the roof, he seizes a shovel and removes a foot or so of it."

The reconstruction of Jack's Henderson cabin shows what it might have looked like.
(Photo: Peter Lourie)

Miners in a cabin eating dinner by candlelight.
(University of Washington Libraries, Special Collections, Hegg 3090)

At night they played checkers and poker, and sometimes chess. Sitting at a hand-hewn spruce table, the men had a hard time drawing cards across the rough surface.

Heat was distributed unevenly in the cabin, too. While the men sat in their undershirts, their faces sweaty from the heat of the roaring stove, the floor was so cold that they wore both wool socks and moccasins. Just eight feet away, on a low shelf by the door, chunks of moose meat and bacon were frozen solid.

When they rested for days in the cabin after coming off the trail or after working hard in the mine shafts, each had to take his turn as cook. The men often teased Jack when it was his turn. They complained about how he boiled the coffee or fried the bacon. They complained about how he baked the ever-present sourdough bread (Everyone made sourdough differently, and it was never made the same way twice).

Jack humorously described how "fickle" sourdough bread could be:

You cannot depend upon it. Still, it is the simplest thing in the world. Make a batter and place it near the stove (that it may not freeze) till it ferments or sours. Then mix the dough with it, and sweeten with soda to taste—of course replenishing the batter for next time. There it is. Was there ever anything simpler? But, oh, the tribulations of the cook! It is never twice the same. If the batter could only be placed away in an equable temperature, all well and good. If one's comrades did not interfere, much vexation of spirit might be avoided. But this cannot be; for Tom fires up the stove till the cabin is become like the hot-room of a Turkish bath; Dick forgets all about the fire till the place is a refrigerator; then along comes Harry and shoves the sour-dough bucket right against the stove to make way for the drying of his mittens. Now heat is a most potent factor in accelerating the fermentation of flour and water, and hence the unfortunate cook is constantly in disgrace with Tom, Dick, and Harry. Last week his bread was yellow from a plethora of soda; this week it is sour from a prudent lack of the same; and next week—ah, who can tell save the god of the fire-box?

Jack made doughnuts fried in bacon grease—the greasier the better. For the men heading out on the trail, foods made with maximum amounts of sugar and grease didn't freeze as easily in severe temperatures, and these doughnuts were easy to carry in pockets. When sugar supplies ran short, Jack just added more bacon grease.

Lack of sugar often made the men tense and grumpy. "Naturally, coffee, and mush, and dried fruit, and rice, eaten without sugar, do not taste exactly as they should." To sweeten the rice, Jack might add some dried fruit. He had to improvise to make bland food taste interesting.

Bacon grease, the ever-present ingredient, was also used to make cabin windows. A sheet of writing paper, "rubbed thoroughly with bacon grease, becomes transparent, sheds water when it thaws, and keeps the cold out and the heat in. In cold weather the ice will form upon the inside of it to the thickness of sometimes two or three inches."

Bacon grease could be used to make candles as well: "When the candles give out, the cook fills a sardine-can with bacon grease, manufactures a wick out of the carpenter's sail-twine, and behold! the slush-lamp stands complete."

Before the men would head out to their claims on Henderson, the cook made "several gallons of beans in the company of numerous chunks of salt pork and much bacon grease. This mess he then molds into blocks of convenient size and places on the roof, where it freezes into bricks in a couple of hours. Thus the men, after a weary day's travel, have but to chop off chunks with an axe and thaw out in the frying-pan."

Jack and his partners were always on the lookout for new ingredients other miners might trade. They took great interest in chili peppers and spices to vary the taste of their endlessly tedious menu of bacon, beans, and bread. "Variety in the grub is as welcome to the men as nuggets," wrote Jack. "When, after eating dried peaches for months, the cook trades a few cupfuls of the same for apricots, the future at once takes on a more roseate hue. Even a change in the brand of bacon will revivify blasted faith in the country."

WORKING THE MINE

TRAVELING IN THE WINTER was rough going in brutal Arctic conditions. In the next five months, Jack would break trail many times to hunt or collect firewood, or visit his Henderson claim from his Stewart cabin. He often hunted with a friend named Elam Harnish (he later gave this name to one of his characters in his novel *Burning Daylight*). But winter mining was usually a solitary business.

Klondike gold is "placer" gold (the *a* is pronounced as in the word *flat*)—loose gold lying in gravel. You take the gravel and wash it, which removes everything else, leaving the heavier gold behind. Winter is a good time to build the shafts and tunnels because the permafrost (soil that is always frozen in the cold regions of the world) keeps the water from flooding the shafts.

The frozen ground had to be thawed with fires, a few feet at a time, to work a four-by-six-foot shaft down into the permafrost. Poor ventilation in the shaft made for dangerous work. If a miner was lucky, he'd get down to bedrock and find a "pay streak," a vein of gold that could be several feet wide, full of gold dust and maybe nuggets, the remains of ancient streams. It might take two months to dig a shaft all the way down to bedrock, a distance of maybe twenty feet.

The miner built a windlass at the top of the crib
and lowered a bucket from a rope to hoist the dirt up and out.
(Photo: Peter Lourie)

Jack started a shaft on his claim. He made many fires in the deepening shaft and dug out the loosening gravel. This was called crib mining because of the crib of logs he built as he dug down to create the main shaft.

Crib mining was time-consuming. You had to be strong to do the work. Buckets of frozen earth called *pay dirt* were continuously dragged up and piled into mounds that would be panned in the spring when the ice melted in the streams and the

Gold miners at work hauling muck to the surface from the shaft. Fire was used to loosen the frozen gravel and make it possible to dig the shaft.
(University of Washington Libraries, Special Collections, UW 28771z)

water ran again. Sometimes in winter the men panned the pay dirt in the warmth of their cabins.

When the shaft got too deep to shovel the muck out, the miner built a windlass at the top of the crib and lowered a bucket from a rope to hoist the dirt up and out.

Miners sift gold in a cabin on Eldorado Creek, Yukon Territory, 1898.
(University of Washington Libraries, Special Collections, A. Curtis 46162)

Day after day, Jack built new fires against the wall of earth to thaw the ice holding the gravel. Those fires took a lot of wood, maybe thirty cords of pine, spruce, and birch. This would usually have been cut the summer before, but Jack didn't have that amount stored up, so it took him four hours a day to collect enough wood. Six hours of burning would thaw only eight inches of frozen muck.

Jack kept shoveling out loose dirt and building new fires, wearing himself out with round-the-clock labor.

It was a hard and simple life. Breakfast over, and they were at work by the first gray light; and when night descended, they did their cooking and camp-chores, smoked and yarned for a while, then rolled up in their sleeping-robes, and slept while the aurora borealis flamed overhead and the stars leaped and danced in the great cold.

During Jack's Arctic winter, the temperatures hovered from −40°F to −50°F for three months with no glimpse of the sun. Jack went through one candle a day down in the shaft, and each one cost as much as $1.50.

❦

TO MOST MINERS, the world of the Arctic winter was deathly depressing, but Jack countered the bleakness through his observations, which he used so well in later stories. Here, in *Burning Daylight*, he describes the weak return of the sun after late January:

It was a dead world, and furthermore, a gray world. The weather was sharp and clear; there was no moisture in the atmosphere, no fog nor haze; yet the sky was a gray pall. The reason for this was that, though there was no cloud in the sky to dim the brightness of day, there was no sun to give brightness. Far to the south the sun climbed steadily to meridian, but between it and the frozen Yukon intervened the bulge of the earth. The Yukon lay in a night shadow, and the day itself was in reality a long twilight. At a quarter before twelve, where a wide bend of the river gave a long vista south, the sun showed its upper rim above the sky-line. But it did not rise perpendicularly. Instead, it rose on a slant, so that by high noon it had barely lifted its lower rim clear of the horizon. It was a dim, wan sun. There was no heat to its rays, and a man could gaze squarely into the full orb of it without hurt to his eyes. No sooner had it reached meridian than it began its slant back beneath the horizon, and at quarter past twelve the earth threw its shadow again over the land.

There were times of no meat through that winter, yet one of the partners was always out looking for moose, wild geese, ducks, and muskrats. One day it would be Sloper, another day Jensen.

Jack himself was not a hunter. He didn't like to kill animals. Walking in the woods, Jack could smell a moose long before he saw the great hulk of the animal grazing in the snow-covered swampy brush.

Back in the small Henderson cabin, Jack got enough light from the makeshift candle, a pitcher of bacon grease with rags in it, to read one of the few books he'd lugged over the Chilkoot. At night when he went visiting in nearby cabins, he always brought his own candle. Another unwritten law of the north was that books were shared. Jack lent out his books.

Emil Jensen said, "Few of us had brought more than one [book], although some had brought as many as three. It was from Jack I borrowed my first book. Anywhere else, I would have passed that thing up without a second thought, but in the Yukon, a book was a book."

London took Jensen on as his own personal student of litera-ture. "Like the master he was, even in those earlier days he set about quietly to convert me to his way of thinking," wrote Emil. Jack inspired his friend to read Darwin's *The Origin of Species*, and he was always quoting lines from poems. He then introduced Emil to Milton's *Paradise Lost* and Kipling's "The Rhyme of the Three Sealers."

Cabin living in the Arctic winter was very good for a writer like Jack. Not only had he always taken a keen interest in people and their stories, now he could observe a variety of men up close. All personal weaknesses sooner or later showed up in the tight quarters of the frozen wilderness. Jack saw the men angry and lonely and starving and sick; he saw them happy and social; and he especially saw them in conflict with one another. There were no secrets in the prospecting camps.

FRIENDSHIPS IN THE COLD

"But no, nothing moved; the Silence crowded in, and the Fear of the North laid icy fingers on his heart."   —"In a Far Country"

"He travels fastest who travels alone . . . but not after the frost has dropped below zero fifty degrees or more."   —Yukon Code

AS THE MINERS returned one by one from Henderson, they clustered in their cabins on Split-Up. Together, they provided the social life that would get them through the long Arctic winter and its incredible silence. Emil Jensen said, "Naturally there was frequent visiting, much talk and careful scheming before we again scattered, some being in favor of one locality and some another. Meanwhile the London cabin was always the centre of attraction. Situated as it was on the bank of the Yukon, all men coming over the long trail must pass it, and the smoke rising white and lazily from its chimney was to all a temptation, for it spoke warmth, and rest, and comfort."

Emil Jensen's friendship was very important to Jack, and the two men seemed to deeply understand and respect each other. Jack's mining companion would form the model for an important character appearing in numerous Klondike stories and known as the Malemute Kid.

Emil Jensen continued:

> Close companionship leaves but little room for secrets. As in a ship on the high seas so it was here in the northern wilderness, all that is in a man must out—the bad with the good, and it is only a question of time when one's innermost thoughts become common property, shared freely with his intimates. And yet nine months constant association with Jack London did not shake the opinion I had formed of his character on that first meeting when he greeted me on the river-bank with the cheery "How do you do? Where from, Friend?" Through the long months he was always the same, a real

friend, helpful, kind and inspiring, always the sunny smile upon his lips.

As well as listening to stories, or telling them, Jack loved a good argument. He would often sit on the edge of his bunk, rolling a cigarette. He smoked continuously and had stains on his fingers from nicotine. One night, Goodman was cooking and Sloper was at work on some carpentry when a man named Bert Hargrave walked in. Jack interrupted the conversation in the cabin to welcome the newcomer with great warm hospitality and a huge smile that put the newcomer at ease.

Hargrave described the young lad's smile "as winsome as a woman's; his brown hair, wavy, almost curly; his clean-cut features and his wonderful eyes. . . . But gentle-hearted and laughter-loving as he was, I have heard him at times—especially when he dwelt upon the unheeded tragedies of industrialism—utter words that stung like a lash."

Some days Jack traveled along the Yukon by dogsled through a frozen landscape. He later described this in *Burning Daylight* as

a world of silence and immobility. Nothing stirred. The Yukon slept under a coat of ice three feet thick. No breath of wind blew. Nor did the sap move in the hearts of the spruce trees that forested the river banks on either hand. The trees, burdened with the last infinitesimal pennyweight of snow their branches could hold, stood in absolute petrifaction. The slightest tremor would have dislodged the snow, and no snow was dislodged. The sled was the one point of life and motion in the midst of the solemn quietude, and the harsh churn of its runners but emphasized the silence through which it moved.

Bert Hargrave partnered with Jack for a bit and, after a winter together, probably knew Jack better than anyone. One day when Hargrave was sick and meat was scarce, Jack and another mining companion, Doc Harvey, broke trail for eighty miles to kill a moose and bring it back to their ailing friend.

Jack was always available to help Emil and others. He often foraged through other cabins to find good reading material for Emil, or he'd assist with the dogs and sleds. He'd even "undertake a two days' hike for plug of tobacco when he saw us restless and grumpy for the want of a smoke."

Once, Jack produced a quart of whiskey he'd been saving, a rare item in the camps, maybe the only such bottle within hundreds of miles. Emil's partner Charlie Borg had broken his ankle while crossing the Chilkoot, and the infected wound now threatened his life.

Doc Harvey had to amputate, so Jack ran to his cabin to fetch the bottle of whiskey he'd kept secret. Only whiskey would make the amputation bearable for patient and doctor alike. Emil Jensen later said, "One quarter of the bottle, or jug, went down [Harvey's] throat to steady his nerves, and the remainder of the whisky saved the life of his patient. . . . Thanks to the benumbing effect of that whisky, my partner survived the butchering, for butchering it was, as cruel as it was necessary." Everyone swigged from the bottle as the patient screamed. Jack didn't flinch.

He heard many yarns in the remote mining camp. One of them was later used in his story "To Build a Fire." A cheechako was traveling one day over a frozen landscape at –70°F. It was so cold that when he spat, the spittle froze instantly in the air with a "sharp, explosive crackle that startled him."

Even though the old-timers in Dawson had said never to travel alone after it dropped to –50°F, the tenderfoot had set out anyway. He should have stopped to make camp. He should have waited for it to warm up. He should have had a partner. If he stepped through the ice of the creek into the water, he'd never get dry by himself.

Jack's main character in the story reaches the juncture of the Stewart and Yukon Rivers before heading up Henderson Creek. He's traveled a few miles and is quite pleased with himself for not freezing to death and thinks he knows more than the old-timers. Then he steps through the ice and gets hopelessly wet. He begins to realize his plight after he tries to make a fire, but such second thoughts are too late. He bares his hands to strike a match, but none of his muscles are working properly and he can't hold the matches, so he puts them in his teeth and tries to light them. He knows that if he can't make a fire, he'll die. A certain fear of death, dull and oppressive, comes to him. With no more matches and no way to make a fire, he knows he's doomed. He runs but falls, and then dies in the snow, realizing the old-timers were right.

The story came from a real-life event. A giant Irishman named Keogh froze to death that winter on the upper Stewart. Bert Hargrave was with Keogh when it happened and surely must have told Jack about it.

Tappan Adney writes about this kind of cold:

Old-timers measure the temperate by the following system . . . : Mercury freezes at −40°; coal-oil (kerosene) freezes at from −35° to −55°, according to grade; "painkiller" freezes at −72°; "St. Jacob's Oil" freezes at −75°; best Hudson's Bay rum freezes at −80°. This last temperature was authoritatively recorded at Fort Reliance, six miles below Dawson; but such low temperatures were rarely observed and did not last more than a few days at a time, during which the old-timer simply stayed in-doors and kept warm.

In the bleakness of winter, the small wooden rooms of the cabins were centers of warmth and good cheer to any who showed up out of the cold. Miners from many countries and walks of life, priests, and Mounties, too, would get together to celebrate holidays. In "To the Man on Trail," Jack's first story published after his return from the Yukon, the men come together to eat and drink, and the character Malemute Kid, gives a toast:

Then Malemute Kid arose, cup in hand, and glanced at the greased-paper window, where the frost stood full three inches thick. "A health to the man on trail this night; may his grub hold out; may his dogs keep their legs; may his matches never miss fire."

In "A Klondike Christmas," Jack captures what it was like to be young and stuck in that little cabin in the wilderness on a holiday. This story begins with the Stampeder writing his mom, then moves into a description of the cozy, warm cabin.

Mouth of the Stuart River,

North West Territory,

December 25, 1897

My dearest Mother:—

Here we are, all safe and sound, and snugly settled down in winter quarters.

Have received no letters yet, so you can imagine how we long to hear from home. We are in the shortest days of the year, and the sun no longer rises, even at twelve o'clock.

Uncle Hiram and Mr. Carter have gone to Dawson to record some placer claims and to get the mail, if there is any. They took the dogs and sled with them, as they had to travel on the ice. We did expect them home for Christmas dinner, but I guess George and I will have to eat alone.

I am to be cook, so you can be sure that we'll have a jolly dinner. We will begin with the staples first. There will be fried bacon, baked beans, bread raised from sour-dough, and—

Living in such close quarters in the gloomy gray of the winter half-light for so many months could also drive miners mad, even to murderous acts.

Once, Jack used Merritt Sloper's ax to chop a hole through the ice to get some water. It was dark, and he chopped hard, not realizing he was chopping into gravel instead of ice, dulling the blade. Sloper became murderously angry, after which Jack moved out of that cabin and into a cabin with Doc Harvey and Bert Hargrave.

Doc Harvey was a popular man in camp, a man of few words.

When he did speak, he always said interesting things, and he really knew how to listen. But living in the close quarters of a small cabin in extreme winter conditions was tough, no matter who your cabinmates were, and relations grew strained even with his closest friends. Jack would later capture the essence of that personal tension and Klondike cabin fever in the story "In a Far Country," when two cabinmates in deep winter descend into hatred until they kill each other.

SCURVY IN THE CREEKS

THERE WERE MANY WAYS to die during the gold rush. Hiking over the Chilkoot with so much gear, Stampeders faced death from the cold, exhaustion, heart attack, bear attack, sickness, flood, and avalanche. Near misses were frequent: people sprained their ankles, broke legs, were scalded by pots of boiling water, got hypothermia, and fell in the Dyea River, etc., etc. It was a dangerous hike. Stampeders died of drowning in lakes, either falling through the ice in the winter or going down with their crude boats in the lakes above Miles Canyon. The Whitehorse Rapids took a few lives. Illnesses like spinal meningitis and tuberculosis took lives, too. Some were murdered by fellow Stampeders, but not as many as one might expect with such a rough group of people undergoing the hardships of the trail and river. A fire in a Dyea bunkhouse took a few lives. In the creeks around Dawson, there was another danger, this one from not having the right foods to eat: scurvy.

As winter wore on, with supplies running short and cabin living feeling more and more cramped, people's personalities were tested to the limit. Some miners couldn't take the harshness as their health deteriorated. One miner from a small creek wrote a letter home, saying, "A man, in order to get along nicely in this country as a prospector, should be in the best health, strong in muscle, of a cheerful disposition, and ready to rough it, with a determination to overcome all obstacles. The man who cannot stand the roughest kind of work ought never to come here." Young Jack in his prime, who everyone said had a cheery and positive disposition, was the kind of person who got along nicely in that country . . . until he came down with scurvy.

Scurvy was also known as the "Klondike plague" or "Arctic leprosy." Caused by a deficiency in vitamin C, scurvy often affected poorly nourished sailors on long voyages, and it ravaged many Stampeders the winter Jack tried to work his mine.

Yukon writer Pierre Berton described the disease:

The legs go lame, the joints ache, the face becomes puffy, the flesh turns soft and pliable as dough, the skin becomes dry and harsh and mottled red, blue, and black. The gums swell and bleed, the teeth rattle in the head and eventually drop out. The breath becomes a stench, the face turns yellow or leaden, and the eyes sink in the skull until the victim, a living skeleton, expires.

That winter, scurvy took the sap out of vibrant Jack London. His constant diet of bacon, beans, and bread, and little or no fresh fruits and vegetables, with their essential vitamin C, wore him down.

"Right leg drawing up," Jack wrote, "can no longer straighten it, even in walking must put my whole weight on toes." The very man who had carried 150-pound loads up the Chilkoot now succumbed to the horrible symptoms. His gums swelled; his teeth were about to fall out. His limbs went numb, and he doubled up like a cripple.

Also, he and his partners had found very little gold (a poor showing of "color"), but they'd found plenty of fool's gold, or iron pyrite, a brassy yellow mineral with a metallic luster that is often mistaken for gold and has no value. Pyrite contains a high percentage of iron and is not an element or metal, but rather an ore. Lucky miners on other creeks were already washing and storing real gold in their cabins. Jack and his partners had no gold to store. Their claims were just not panning out.

Only Fred Thompson kept thinking he'd strike it rich. Maintaining his aloof yet gentlemanly demeanor, he was the one partner who refused to admit defeat. "I just know we're going to strike it rich, and very soon!" he said. Some of the men thought he was arrogant, but only Fred held fast to his vision of striking it big on Henderson. He never did find his golden stash, though he kept looking long after the others had given up.

By Christmas, Jack and his Henderson pals were "thoroughly disillusioned." Yet Jack's optimistic friend Emil later wrote that "we were young, and we had gained much in the way of experience; and our muscles had grown hard as nails." Emil continued, "Looking at it from every angle but the one for which we had come, and for which we had endured so much, it proved all that I . . . could have wished for."

Jack lost a lot of weight. He was like a stick with clothes, but he also remained extremely resilient. He began to think he might now have the raw material for some magazine articles and essays. Although he hadn't kept a journal in the Klondike, his passion for writing had never left him.

One day, Jack stepped outside and carved a blaze in a spruce tree near the cabin. A local trapper passing by asked why he'd put the mark in the tree. Weak from scurvy, Jack nevertheless replied with the confidence of a timber wolf, "Because someday I'll make my mark as a writer."

Back inside the stove-steamy cabin, Jack stood and grabbed a pencil in his gloved hand. Though he was weak, he began to write firmly on a log near his bunk five feet from the floor, holding the pencil the way a painter holds a paintbrush, with thumb and forefinger stretched out along the pencil. He scratched into the wood these words: *Jack London, miner, author, Jan 27 1898.*

PART FIVE

MARCH–JULY 1898

HEADING HOME DOWN THE LONG YUKON RIVER

ICE BREAKUP AND LEAVING THE WHITE SILENCE

WALKING THROUGH THE WOODS in March and April, Jack heard the trees explode like gunshots in the frozen silence. After a couple of warm days, sap would rise in the spruce saplings; then a cold wave would plunge them back into a deep freeze, and the trees would just snap.

Outside, the snow kept flying through late winter—a hard, fine, dry snow, "more like sugar. Kick it, and it flew with a hissing noise like sand. There was no cohesion among the particles, and it could not be molded into snow-balls. It was not composed of flakes, but of crystals—tiny, geometrical frost-crystals. In truth, it was not snow, but frost."

In the Arctic gloom, Jack heard the huskies crying to the moon, as he later wrote in a nonfiction essay for *Harper's Weekly* called "Husky: The Wolf-Dog of the North."

> When the frost grows bitter and the aurora-borealis trails its cold fires across the heavens, they voice their misery to the night. Heartbreaking, sobbing, it rises like a wail of lost and tortured souls, and when a thousand huskies are in full chorus it is as though the roof had tumbled in and hell stood naked to the stars.

Well into April, the sun lingered longer in the sky, setting farther to the west. At the end of the month, the days stretched out for hours. Snow began to melt. Invisible streams moved under the snow. "Tiny white snow-birds appeared from the south, lingered a day, and resumed their journey into the north. Once, high in the air, looking for open water and ahead of the season, a wedged squadron of wild geese honked northward. And down by the river bank a clump of dwarf willows burst into bud."

Panning for gold
(Museum of History & Industry, shs11388)

Now water everywhere was moving again, and life flooded back into the lifeless earth. When May arrived, Jack wrote:

last-year's mosquitoes, full-grown but harmless, crawled out of rock crevices and rotten logs. More and more geese and ducks flew overhead. And still the river held. By May tenth, the ice of the Stewart, with a great rending and snapping, tore loose from the banks and rose three feet. But it did not go down-stream. The lower Yukon, up to where the Stewart flowed into it, must first break and move on. Until then the ice of the Stewart could only rise higher and higher on the increasing flood beneath. When the Yukon would break was problematical. Two thousand miles away it flowed into Bering Sea, and it was the ice conditions of Bering Sea that would determine when the Yukon could rid itself of the millions of tons of ice that cluttered its breast.

Some parties traveling on the river's sun-weakened ice just disappeared into the water through invisible openings. Whole dog teams fell through and were never seen again.

On into the summer, when the earth around the streams thawed, the prospectors emerged from the caves of their cabins to work outside and in the shafts. Fighting off hordes of attacking mosquitoes, they built dams along the creeks to channel the water for washing the gold out of the muck they drew from the shafts.

Now Jack witnessed firsthand the terrifying drama of Yukon spring breakup.

The down-stream movement began at five in the morning. . . . The ice tore by, great cakes of it caroming against the bank, uprooting trees, and gouging out earth by hundreds of tons. All about them the land shook and reeled from the shock of these tremendous collisions. At the end of an hour the run stopped. Somewhere below it was blocked by a jam. Then the river began to rise, lifting the ice on its breast till it was higher than the bank. From behind ever more water bore down, and ever more millions of tons of ice added their weight to the congestion. The pressures and stresses became terrific. Huge cakes of ice were squeezed out till they popped into the air like melon seeds squeezed from between the thumb and forefinger of a child, while all along the banks a wall of ice was forced up. When the jam broke, the noise of grinding and smashing redoubled. For another hour the run continued. The river fell rapidly. But the wall of ice on top the bank, and extending down into the falling water, remained.

For the first time since November, Jack saw open water.

Bert Hargrave had already gone down to Dawson before river breakup to be treated for his own scurvy. Jack's other cabinmate, Doc Harvey, said it was now time for Jack to get out, too, not only to head down to Dawson for treatment in the hospital, but maybe to leave the Yukon altogether. The only problem was that with so much broken ice cluttering the river, leaving now would be a treacherous game. Doc said it was necessary; Jack was in bad shape.

So even though it would have been safer to leave a few weeks later, when the Yukon River was clear of ice, he and Doc Harvey prepared for the journey. Doc helped Jack dismantle their cabin in order to build a raft. Jack was mostly limp. His movements were slow and he fumbled, panting from weakness.

They launched their raft into the river, and Jack's head swam as he tried to get his balance in the swift and jolting current. Together they fought off the ice using poles and pushed off sandbars until they reached Dawson, where they sold the wood from the raft for six hundred dollars.

Jack spent his half of the money on good food and medical attention at the hospital.

DAWSON ONE LAST TIME

SPENDING HIS LAST THREE WEEKS in the Yukon with his pal Emil Jensen was a good way to end his Arctic adventure. Jensen wrote, "Jack camped with me and my mate in our tent at Dawson. If there had been trouble between them [his original three partners] I did not know it, for he did not complain, and I did not ask. 'Our food gave out,' he said simply."

"The Last Turn" in the Exchange. May 31, 12 P.M. 1901.
Scene in a Dawson Gambling house.

Jack loved the lively saloons and gambling houses of Dawson.
(University of Washington Libraries, Special Collections, UW6624)

*A horse-drawn cart hauling lumber gets
stuck in the mud on Front Street, Dawson.*
(University of Washington Libraries, Special Collections, Hegg 3094)

Jack found some relief from his scurvy in the vitamin C of a
type of beer flavored with spruce shavings. Soon he was strong
enough to get a little work picking up driftwood logs with a
rowboat. He started to visit the dance halls and saloons again.
After so many months without alcohol, he returned happily to
his drinking ways.

Unusual flooding that spring turned the streets to a nightmare of mud. Horses and men stumbled through the black slime.
Jack crawled from gambling den to dance hall. He could walk the
high, narrow boardwalk that lined both sides of the street until
he had to get across the mud to reach another saloon.

FATHER JUDGE
AND HIS HOSPITAL

ALL OVER DAWSON, penniless men and women were dying of pneumonia, malaria, typhoid, dysentery, starvation, and scurvy. "Get out of town" was common advice. If the Stampeders didn't have the money or resources to spend

Many Stampeders were buried in a graveyard above Dawson.
You can visit those graves today.

(Photos: Peter Lourie)

another long winter there, they were warned to go quickly. New and untested gold seekers might arrive one day, sell what they had, and leave the next day. Others had no choice but to work for the miners who had claims, like Big Alec, who paid sixteen dollars a day for hired hands.

Some hardy ones stayed long after the Stampede ended in 1899. These often found work at their previous trades and made new lives for themselves. When they died in Dawson, their graves were marked with a simple wooden marker in the cemetery above the town. Those graves are still there.

St. Mary's, a log hospital, was founded in the summer of 1897 by a Catholic priest named Father William Henry Judge. Dawson residents called him the Saint of Dawson because of his relentless care for sick and dying Stampeders. For fifty dollars, you could get a ticket that allowed you to be admitted into the hospital anytime for up to a whole year.

The Jesuit priest befriended Jack and strongly advised him to get out of Dawson as soon as he could. The scurvy couldn't be cured otherwise, he said. He also told Jack about an incident that had happened to him along the trail when he spent hours in sub-zero weather trying to make a fire to fight off frostbite. The priest apparently fell through the ice on the Yukon. With wet feet, he pushed forward, thinking he could reach his cabin nearby. Two hours later, when he found the cabin, he tried starting a fire in the stove but had to go back down to his sled to get a candle as he was having difficulty lighting matches. He thought a lit candle might more easily start the stove. His hands were so frozen that he had to use his elbows to pull himself up from the ground. Jack added parts of the priest's experience to what he'd learned about the Irishman Keogh when he wrote the short story "To Build a Fire."

Originally from Baltimore, Father Judge arrived in the Yukon in 1894 and established a mission in the early mining town of Forty Mile. When gold was found on Bonanza Creek, he moved to Dawson in March 1897, where he began to treat patients in a tent, then in his newly constructed hospital, which Big Alec had helped pay for. Father Judge supplied food and shelter and medicine to prospectors, including Jack. Judge was so loved that when he died of pneumonia in 1899 at the age of forty-nine, his funeral was the largest Dawson had ever seen.

SHOVING OFF

IN EARLY JUNE, the sun never dips below the horizon—that's why it's the "land of the midnight sun." It's daylight all summer long.

Soon, the big riverboats, which had been stuck for months in winter ice, would move upriver again. They'd disgorge hundreds of ever-hopeful gold seekers. More than likely, these cheechakos would meet the same misfortune as Jack—if not scurvy, then dysentery, frostbite, or starvation. Certainly, their chances of striking it rich were infinitesimal.

Masses of other gold seekers arrived the way Jack and his friends had come, from the Alaskan coast by way of the Chilkoot and White Pass Trails. With the spring thaw, the hordes were on the move from Lake Laberge and beyond.

When the ice broke and the Yukon flowed again, steamboats carrying thousands of cheechakos came up the long river to Dawson.
(University of Washington Libraries, Special Collections, Hegg 740A)

The June 1898 inaugural issue of Dawson's *Yukon Midnight Sun* newspaper ran a front-page story entitled "Gold Output for the Year: Twenty Millions." It explained, "Not more than twenty-five claims on Eldorado have been extensively worked. During the winter, while drifting was going on, very little thorough prospecting for the purpose of determining the value of the gravel was done." And so on.

On June 8, Jack said good-bye to his pals Hargrave, Harvey, and Jensen. They looked on with envy as Jack and two other friends dropped into a small boat and left the Yukon on another adventure, poling for the river's mouth at St. Michaels. A brisk six-mile-an-hour current sucked at the little vessel. Jack "turned about for a final glimpse of Dawson—dreary, desolate Dawson, built in a swamp, flooded to the second story, populated by dogs, mosquitoes and gold-seekers. Our friends attempted a half-hearted cheer, and filled the air with messages for those at home."

Emil Jensen remembered the day Jack left town, with so many miles to drift, sick with scurvy, but also "sick with the failure consciousness that had gripped so many, and yet, as I bade him farewell, the well-known boyish, engaging smile took the sting out of our parting, though it haunts me still."

When he'd taken Emil's hand, Jack had said, "I shall be glad, Emil, when some day next summer I shall open my door and find you waiting on the porch."

With the June sun blazing above, Jack said good-bye to the Klondike, a place that would define him as a writer of the Arctic north, of wolves, sled dogs, and gold seekers. Some say Jack London went north for gold but left with great stories percolating inside him. He'd certainly explored a remarkable region at a notable time in history. In the Arctic, Jack had lived among people from different backgrounds, real people that he could now mold into fictional characters.

On that day in 1898, he must have felt a great release, not just from sickness and cabin fever, and not from disappointment, but because he was excited to know he finally had the inspiration and material he needed to become a published writer. When he set his boat adrift in the powerful current of the mighty Yukon for the long journey to the Bering Sea, how could he not feel a release from the harshness of winter, from scurvy, and from not finding any gold?

Later he wrote:

> Our boat was home-made, weak-kneed and leaky, but in thorough harmony with the wilderness we were traversing. A smooth and polished creation of the boat-builder's art might have been more beautiful, but we were quite agreed that it would have been less comfortable and a positive discord to our rough-hewn environment. In the bow was the wood shed, while amidships, built of pine boughs and blankets, was the bed chamber. Then came the rower's bench, and jammed between this and the steersman was our snug little kitchen. It was a veritable home, and we had little need of going ashore, save out of curiosity or to lay in a fresh supply of firewood.

Twenty-three days after leaving Dawson, Jack and his boat mates arrived at the mouth of the Yukon. In the vast delta, Jack saved a French-Italian priest named Robeau who was in danger of capsizing in his kayak. Taking the priest aboard, Jack found the man to be a kindred spirit, one of the most interesting characters, he said, that he'd met in the Arctic. Robeau had been in Alaska working on an Inuit grammar book for twelve years. Even as he departed, Jack was soaking up details and finding characters to create. He always loved meeting people, asking them questions and listening closely to their stories.

He found work shoveling coal on a steamer headed for Port Townsend, Washington. He was still weak from scurvy, but he managed to earn passage money for a boat from there to San Francisco.

HOME

1898–1899

CAPTURING THE KLONDIKE IN STORIES

FINALLY HOME IN THE FALL of 1898—the whole trip had taken him just one year—Jack recovered from the effects of scurvy but felt the pain of losing his stepfather. John London had left him a fifteen-dollar overcoat, which Jack had to pawn for two dollars. Jack still had no money.

Feverishly, he began to write story after story, mostly Klondike tales, some nonfiction and poetry. He continued to struggle to get published even as he looked for work. He mailed his stories to magazines, only to have publishers reject them. Each time Jack saw the self-addressed stamped envelope that he had included with his submissions, he knew it was another rejection. But he didn't give up.

He applied to work for the US Postal Service. He even sold his only treasure from the Klondike—$4.50 worth of genuine Yukon gold dust. When the old wanderlust came over him again, he tried his hand at prospecting once more, this time in Nevada. He failed and returned home to write more stories and receive more rejections.

Jack remained hopeful and resilient. He'd read somewhere that a writer could make ten dollars for a thousand words, so he pounded out words, but his stories were rejected many times.

Then came his big break. *Overland Monthly*, a respected literary journal that published Mark Twain, offered Jack five dollars for "To the Man on Trail." A whole week's wage. Never mind that they didn't pay him for months. Then another story was accepted in the *Black Cat*, for which they would pay him a whopping sum of forty dollars. The editor said it was that good! (Remember, $40 in 1897 would be $1,120 in today's dollars!)

In June 1899, less than a year after returning from the Klondike, Jack was asked to cut a twelve-thousand-word manuscript for the *Atlantic Monthly*. He didn't like the idea of cutting at all, but managed to whittle it down to ten thousand words, and a few months later, his literary reputation and financial success were sealed when his story "An Odyssey of the North" appeared in the January 1900 issue of the magazine. He now knew he could publish with the best of them, and his writing career began to take off.

———◆———

MAYBE, IN THE END, Jack London is the only King of the Klondike. Carmack, Keish (Skookum Jim) and Káa Goox (Dawson Charlie), along with a few hundred other Stampeders, did get rich. Mighty rich. A lucky few managed to hold on to their riches to pass along to their families. Most Eldorado Kings, though, like Big Alec McDonald, squandered their loot and died penniless.

Although Jack was never good with money and probably could not have been the shrewd businessman he thought he might be, he did pass along to the world his own kind of Klondike gold. He produced ten published short stories in a single year, for which he was paid a mere $7.50 apiece. Only two years after he left Dawson, at twenty-four years old, Jack published his first book, a collection of eight Klondike tales, *The Son of the Wolf.*

Jack in 1903 when The Call of the Wild *was published.*
(Photo JLP 210, Jack London Papers, the Huntington Library,
San Marino, California)

Jack's career as a writer would soar the way he'd always imagined. With the publication of *The Call of the Wild* in 1903, at the age of twenty-seven, Jack became the most famous and highly paid writer in the world.

After returning from the Klondike, he continued to write a thousand words a day, which is like the hard work of placer mining, sifting the literary gold from the loose gravel of raw experience.

Perhaps the metaphor works. You build a fire to thaw the frozen ground and then you scrape out a few feet of loose gravel, and then you build another fire and scrape down again. You dig for twenty frozen feet until you reach bedrock and, with luck, also the pay streak.

White Fang and *The Call of the Wild* and "To Build a Fire" and "The White Silence" are Jack's pay streak. In more than fifty Klondike short stories and novels, he painted powerful scenes and drew unforgettable characters from his experiences living the Stampede. Jack took back gold from the Yukon, but not in physical form. His gold—and ours—is in the stories of the people he met along this amazing Arctic journey.

AFTERWORD

WHEN I VISITED Dawson on a recent summer, Dawne Mitchell, curator of the Jack London Museum, drove me to the north edge of town to the spot where Jack had pitched his tent near the Bond cabin in the fall of 1897. For years, this side of town had been used as a garbage dump, but now it was clear and open. Father Judge's hospital would have been only yards from Jack's tent.

Dawne and I found fresh bear scat in the brush that kept us alert. We had no gun or bear spray. We walked to the grave of Father Judge, where a monument was erected to the man who convinced Jack to get medical attention for his own good.

My visit to Dawson happened to coincide with the biannual festival of the First Nation tribe of the Tr'ondëk Hwëch'in (Hän) in the village of Moosehide, three miles downriver. At the Dawson beach in the cold summer rain, a gang of dogs was messing about as I waited for a boat to go to the opening ceremony at Moosehide. The villagers had moved their residence three miles downriver to Moosehide just after Jack left the Klondike. They'd moved to get some peace and quiet after being squeezed out of Tr'ochëk by the Stampeders.

In the rain, I imagined riverboats arriving in June of 1898 with crates of fresh vegetables and hundreds of gold-crazed

Stampeders, along with their outfits. Riverboats actually ran along the Yukon until 1956, but Jack's cabin on Split-Up long ago fell into the river from erosion.

The *Klondike Nugget* in Dawson published this note around the time Jack departed on a raft with fellow Henderson Creek prospectors Charley Taylor and John Thorson.

THE NEWCOMER IN DAWSON

There are many men in Dawson at the present time who feel keenly disappointed. They have come thousands of miles on a perilous trip, risked life, health and property, spent months of the most arduous labor a man can perform, and at length with expectations raised to the highest pitch have reached the coveted goal only to discover the fact that there is nothing here for them.

On an even more negative note, one character from London's novel *Burning Daylight* described what the Klondike would look like in a few years, after so many miners had ravaged the land around Bonanza and El Dorado Creeks. Greed is not pretty:

It was a scene of a vast devastation. The hills, to their tops, had been shorn of trees, and their naked sides showed signs of goring and perforating that even the mantle of snow could not hide. Beneath him, in every direction, were the cabins of men. But not many men were visible. A blanket of smoke filled the valleys and turned the gray day to melancholy twilight. Smoke arose from

> a thousand holes in the snow, where, deep down on bed-rock, in the frozen muck and gravel, men crept and scratched and dug, and ever built more fires to break the grip of the frost. . . . Figures of men crawled out of the holes, or disappeared into them. . . . The wreckage of the spring washing appeared everywhere . . . all the debris of an army of gold-mad men.

After Jack left Dawson, some of his partners stayed on. Fred Thompson worked as a customs broker until 1913, when he returned to Santa Rosa, California, to resume his old job as court reporter. Big Jim Goodman, joined by his brother, Dan, raised a family and opened a hardware store in town, in a building that still stands today. A sign out front says GUNS, AMMUNITION, HARDWARE, TOBACCO, FURNITURE, GROCERY, CLOTHING, TENTS. Dan lived above the store. He brought his daughter, Zella, to the Yukon, where she danced, sang, and played the piano for silent movies that were shown in the saloons. Some say that even today you

*Mining claims, Eldorado Creek 1898.
Mining for gold can devastate the
streams and the land around them.*
(University of Washington Libraries,
Special Collections, Hegg 792)

can hear her singing when you walk past the tumbledown building that was her home. The Goodman brothers prospected and operated various businesses in the Yukon and Alaska from 1897 to 1922.

Martin Tarwater split off from the group when they first got to Dawson and later died of acute asthma in 1898. Merritt Sloper left the Klondike the same summer as Jack. When he returned home to San Francisco, his wife filed for divorce because he had not struck it rich.

Father Judge's hospital burned to the ground for a second time in February 1950 and was never rebuilt.

———•———

IN 1900, just after his first collection of Klondike stories was published, Jack got a letter from Cornelius M. Gepfert, another pal from Split-Up Island. In his reply, Jack's letter recalls the old days (three years before!) and talks about how he'd had to "modify" some things from the Klondike in order to make fiction:

> Have you read my book "The Son of the Wolf"? They are all Klondike stories, collected, and I am busy wondering how the Klondikers, who know all about it, will take them. If you read them, tell me what you think of them, and don't be chary of whatever adverse criticism comes into your mind. You see, I have had to take liberties, and to idealize, etc. etc. for the sake of the artistic effect, and often from the inherent need of the tales themselves, and for their literary value.

Jack London died on November 22, 1916, at the age of forty, of a stroke and heart failure. His body had taken a beating throughout his life, and it finally just gave out at his ranch in California, which he'd worked for many years.

His adventurous life spanned the history of the United States between the Civil War and World War I. He witnessed the great technological revolutions of the telephone, the moving picture, the airplane, and the automobile. Although it was a short life by today's standards, never has anyone lived a fuller four decades than did Jack London. Perhaps Jack's pal from the mining camp best described his passion for life. Nearly thirty years after they'd been together at Stewart River, Emil Jensen captured Jack's desire for learning:

> Monotony found no place to light in Jack London's make-up. The little as well as the big things in our daily life held for him, always, a stimulus that made his every waking hour worth living. To him, there was in all things something new, something alluring, something worth while, be it a game of whist, an argument, or the sun at noonday glowing cold and brilliant above the hills to the south. He was ever on tiptoe with expectancy, whether silent with wondering awe, as on a night when we saw the snows aflame beneath a weird, bewildering sky or in the throes of a frenzied excitement while we watched a mighty river at flood tide, and the ice "go out" in the moonlight.

Jack died young, but during his brief time in the Klondike, he did find his gold—in the land he loved, in the creeks, on the trails, in the muddy streets of Dawson, and in the dogs and Stampeders who inspired his world-famous stories and novels.

Perhaps it is fitting to let Emil Jensen have the last word. Emil says:

He is gone now. But the world remembers. I, too, remember. Not because of the greatness that the world has recognized, nor because of the achievements that startled a skeptical world, but because there are depths stirred within me when I recall the curly-headed boy I learned to love in the cold and silent Northland.

NOTES FROM THE AUTHOR

TO TELL THIS TALE I've taken a few liberties. We have no direct record of how much mining Jack did on Henderson Creek, or how much dogsledding experience he had, or how he actually felt and what he actually saw during his Klondike adventure. Much of what we know about Jack's experience comes through the prolific writing he did after he returned to California, from his wife's and daughter's books about him, and from the memories of those who were with him in the creeks. In this telling, I have Jack do a few things that he may or may not have done. For instance, we don't know if he confronted a wolf, and we don't know how many wolves he saw. He could easily have seen more than one. When I was in Dawson a few years ago, I stood before the magnificent creature early in the morning right at the mouth of Bonanza Creek. Certainly Jack and the other miners could have had any of the experiences I attempt to capture in this book. The object of my tale is to convey the spirit and drama of the Klondike Stampeders as much as the amazing history of that wild time. I believe I have kept this tale well within the realm of the possible. And if I can inspire just one of my readers to have his or her own adventure in the great outdoors, then I will have accomplished what I set out to do.

A FEW THOUGHTS ON
THE NOTION OF WILDERNESS

THE TRIBES OF THE COAST and the interior of Alaska and the Yukon, now collectively known as the First Nations, did exist—and still do—as their own civilization in the Yukon. Therefore, "raw" and "wilderness" are not factual descriptions of the place but our own cultural constructs. To keep in the spirit of Jack London's own writing, I use these words to describe how the Stampeders saw the terrain.

The Klondike is a fast and shallow stream, long known as an excellent salmon fishing river in the Yukon. The point of land between the Klondike and Yukon Rivers is the heart of the traditional territory of the First Nations Tr'ondëk Hwëch'in tribe (literally "People of the Klondike" or "People of the River"), sometimes referred to as Hän. For hundreds of years, families gathered

there to fish for salmon, hunt moose up the Klondike Valley, and meet, feast, and trade. *Klondike* comes from *thronduick* (or *tr'ondëk*), a Native Hän word meaning "hammerstone," a tool used to hammer down stakes for setting salmon traps.

George Carmack
(Yukon Archives, James Albert Johnson fonds, 82/341, #14)

George Carmack's wife, Shaaw Tláa (Kate Carmack), her brother Keish (Skookum Jim), and nephew Káa Goox (Dawson Charlie) were members of the Tagish tribe. The names Dawson "Tagish" Charlie and Skookum Jim Mason are their "white" names, given to them because the Europeans usually could not pronounce their real names.

Keish (Skookum Jim Mason) at his mine on Bonanza Creek

(National Park Service, Klondike Gold Rush National Historical Park, Candy Waugaman Collection, KLGO Library DP-116-10570)

Káa Goox (Dawson "Tagish" Charlie)

(MacBride Museum of Yukon History Collection 1989.1.004)

Kate Carmack and George Carmack pose with their daughter,
Graphie, in front of their log cabin on Bonanza Creek, 1897.
(Yukon Archives, James Albert Johnson fonds, 82/341 #15)

MAKING A CLAIM

THE FIRST STEP for a miner arriving in the Klondike was to find sufficient gold to warrant staking a claim. You did that by going up or down a stream panning along the way (as Jack and his partners did when they first arrived at Henderson Creek), and if you found gold in significant quantities, you blazed a nearby tree and wrote on it something along the lines of what George Carmack wrote: *To whom it may concern—I do, this day, locate and claim, by right of discovery, five hundred feet, running up stream from this notice. Located this 17th day of August, 1896 G. W. Carmack.*

Then you paced five hundred feet upstream and posted a second similar notice. If you didn't have a nearby tree, you took along wooden stakes to drive into the ground—thus, you *staked your claim.* The first to make a claim on a stream (called the discovery claim) was entitled to two claims, or one thousand feet along a stream. Subsequent claims were numbered depending on how far above or below the discovery claim they were (one above, two below, etc). Then, of course, you went into town to register your claim. Before Dawson was a town, prospectors had to go downriver to Forty Mile, where there was a claim office.

The actual size of each claim varied depending on the terrain. Generally, valleys are wider at the mouth of a stream than at the stream's beginning, so claim sizes would be bigger at the stream

George Carmack on his discovery claim, 1898
(Yukon Archives, James Albert Johnson fonds, 82/341 #19)

mouth. That might not mean much because the richest concentrations of gold could be anywhere along the stream. In the Klondike, the richest gold findings were at the junction of Eldorado and Bonanza Creeks. The real problem with the initial discovery on Bonanza Creek was that everybody's pace was different, and so one man's 500 feet might actually have been 489 feet or perhaps 507 feet, or some other figure. This caused huge problems when claims were officially surveyed with instruments; all sorts of discrepancies were found, and miners had to make lots of adjustments. It was a mess.

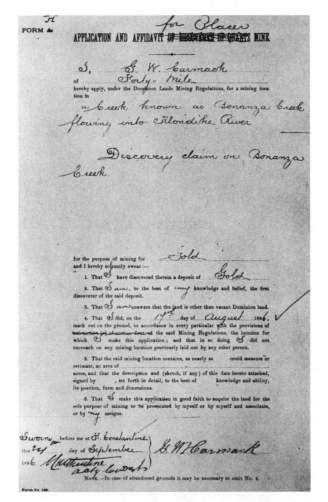

Application filed by George Carmack when he recorded his discovery claim on Bonanza Creek, 1896

(University of Washington Libraries, Special Collections, UW 2747)

BOOKS ABOUT JACK LONDON IN THE KLONDIKE

THREE GOOD BOOKS have been written about Jack London in the Klondike, any one of which would make a fine follow-up source for students interested in how Jack's writing ties into his Klondike adventure: Franklin Walker's *Jack London and the Klondike*, Mike Wilson's *Jack London's Klondike Adventure*, and Dick North's *Sailor on Snowshoes: Tracking Jack London's Northern Trail*. This last one is an exciting yarn of how Dick himself believes he found the cabin up Henderson Creek where Jack carved his name into a log in January 1898, then how Dick and friends brought that very cabin, log by log, back to Dawson in the Yukon Territory of Canada and to Oakland, California. In fact, half of the original logs were used for building a replica in Oakland, California; the other half for building a second replica in Dawson, honoring both Jack's California home and his adventure home in the north.

A FEW FINAL INSIGHTS

THERE'D ALWAYS BEEN another side of Jack, a softer, more sensitive side. From the age of six, he loved to read books yet had little time for reading, due to chores and work. As a reader, he lived partly in an imaginary world of literature. In his spare time, he dreamed of adventures and romance in far-off places.

Even as a child, he had a restless spirit. He loved to read the adventure tales of explorers such as Captain Cook and Francisco Pizarro.

When he was eight, he read Washington Irving's *The Alhambra*, a collection of tales and sketches about Moorish Spain. Jack built a replica of the Alhambra, the Moorish palace in Granada. At the Cole Grammar School in Oakland, he often sat reading a book during recess instead of playing ball. One day a bully teased him and threw Jack's book on the ground. Jack got up and bloodied the boy's face. The bully never bothered him again.

And what exactly is an oyster pirate? Why was it so profitable? The oyster industry of San Francisco Bay relied on the Southern Pacific Railway leasing its lands (the tidal flats area off San Mateo) to commercial oyster growers. The public was not happy that the railway company had a monopoly over the industry (a monopoly is when a group has exclusive control over a service or commodity). When only one company controls a business, it can drive prices too high, and this is what happened with oysters. The so-called pirates who raided the oyster beds at night and sold their loot in the morning had the sympathy of the public because they could sell their oysters at a much lower cost. The pirates made fast money (Jack said he made one hundred and eighty dollars in a twelve-hour period), but they also had to take chances.

After about a year, when it started getting too dangerous to be an oyster pirate (competition among pirates had grown stiff since more and more people were entering the lucrative business),

Jack cleverly traded sides and joined the California Fish Patrol. Now he could get paid for his skills in a boat as well as for his pirate knowledge even as he protected the very oyster beds he'd just been raiding. He operated in a different part of the bay so that he didn't arrest any of his former pals.

NOTABLE PLACES

Bennett, Bennett City—Settlement on Lake Bennett, thirty-three miles above Dyea on the Chilkoot Trail, where Stampeders constructed boats for the Yukon River journey to the Klondike.

Chilkoot Trail—A traditional transportation route through rugged mountain terrain, connecting the Pacific Coast of Alaska with the upper Yukon River in British Columbia. It is best known as the route used by thousands of prospectors on their way to the Yukon gold fields during the gold rush of 1896–1898.

Dawson City—Town site laid out by Joseph Ladue and Arthur Harper at the confluence of the Yukon and Klondike Rivers in 1896, and named for Canadian geologist George Dawson.

Dyea—Boomtown at the foot of the Chilkoot Trail on the Alaskan coast.

Fort Selkirk—Trading post established in 1848 by Robert Campbell of the Hudson's Bay Co., at the junction of the Pelly and Lewes Rivers. The post was burned down a few years later by Tlingit traders who did not appreciate the competition.

Golden Stairs—The 1,500 or so steps carved and worn into the ice up Chilkoot Pass in the winter of 1897–1898.

Happy Camp—A popular camping spot twenty-one miles

above Dyea on the Chilkoot Trail, and four miles from Lake Lindeman.

Klondike—Gold district encompassing the Klondike River and its tributaries. The name comes from the corruption of the Hän (Tr'ondëk Hwëch'in) word meaning hammerstone, which was used to hammer down stakes to set salmon traps.

Lindeman, Lindeman City—Settlement at the start of the Yukon River headwaters on Lake Lindeman.

Miles Canyon—Mile-long, Upper Yukon canyon named in 1883 by Lieutenant Frederick Schwatka in honor of his military expedition sponsor, General Nelson Miles.

Moosehide Slide—The landmark depression or scar on the mountain rising above Dawson. (The Hän village downstream from Dawson is also called Moosehide.)

Scales—A settlement at the foot of the Golden Stairs, where steelyard scales were used by professional packers who made a business of toting freight to the summit. As the gold rush developed, the Scales hosted a small tent city, including six restaurants, two hotels, a saloon, and many freighting offices and warehouses.

Sheep Camp—Major boomtown thirteen miles from Dyea on the Chilkoot Trail, and the jumping-off point for pack trips over the Chilkoot Pass. Called Sheep Camp because it may have served as headquarters for men hunting mountain sheep.

Stewart Island—There were actually multiple islands just below the mouth of the Stewart River. The one Jack and his partners wintered on was probably called "Upper" Island or

"Split-Up" Island because it was a place where partners often split to go their separate ways. I have simplified the nomenclature to Stewart Island, as Dick North does in *Sailor on Snowshoes: Tracking Jack London's Northern Trail.*

White Pass Trail—Also known as the Dead Horse Trail, the forty-two-mile trail scratched out of the woods and rocks and touted as a pack trail to the Yukon River headwaters (also ending at Lake Bennett), in competition with the Chilkoot Trail from nearby Dyea. More than three thousand pack animals perished on this route during the height of the rush.

Yukon Territory—Formed in 1898 from the Northwest Territories in Canada, 205,346 square miles in size, with the territorial capital relocated from Dawson to Whitehorse in 1953. The name Yukon comes from the Athabascan word *yukona*, meaning "great river," which was recorded by Hudson's Bay traders in the 1840s.

JACK LONDON'S WRITING

This is not a complete list of London's Klondike stories, but it's a good place to start—in particular where I have put a star after the work.

NOVELS

The Call of the Wild *
White Fang *
Burning Daylight
Smoke Bellew

SHORT STORIES

"To Build a Fire"*
"The White Silence"*
"The Men of Forty-Mile"*
"In a Far Country"*
"To the Man on Trail"*
"The Law of Life"*
"The League of Old Men"*
"A Klondike Christmas"*
"The Night-Born"*
"The Son of the Wolf"
"The One Thousand Dozen"*

"The Wisdom of the Trail"
"Bâtard"
"Love of Life"
"The Story of Keesh"
"All Gold Canyon"
"Up the Slide"*
"Trust"*

NONFICTION

"The Gold Hunters of the North"*
"Through the Rapids on the Way to the Klondike"*
"From Dawson to the Sea"*
"Economics in the Klondike"
"The Husky"*
"Housekeeping in the Klondike"*

JACK LONDON TIME LINE

1876
Born January 12 at 615 Third Street, San Francisco, California.

1879
John London, Jack's stepfather, moved his family to Oakland, California, where John operated a vegetable garden on a parcel of land near the present Emeryville.

1881
Started grade school in Alameda, California.

Jack London as a boy, about 1882

(JLP 518 Alb. 80 #10198, Jack London papers, the Huntington Library, San Marino, California)

1883
John London moved his family to the Tobin Ranch in San Mateo County, California, where they raised a few horses and planted potatoes.

1885
Jack, also called "Johnny," discovered the world of books and read Washington Irving's *The Alhambra*.

1886
The family bought a house in Oakland after living on farms in San Mateo County and Livermore. Jack discovered that the Oakland public library would supply him with books. He met librarian Ina Coolbrith, who helped him choose the right books for his inquisitive mind.

1887
Enrolled at the Cole Grammar School in West Oakland.

1891
Graduated from Cole Grammar School (eighth grade). Obtained a steady job in a salmon cannery at ten cents an hour. He borrowed money to buy the sloop *Razzle-Dazzle* and became an oyster pirate on San Francisco Bay.

1892
Became a member of the Fish Patrol and stayed in Benicia, California.

1893
Signed on as able-bodied seaman on the *Sophia Sutherland*, a three-masted sealing schooner, and served eight months. Came home to write "Typhoon Off the Coast of Japan," which won first prize ($25) in a local newspaper's literary contest. It was the first story ever written by Jack London for publication.

Jack London, sailor, about 1893
(JLP 170, Jack London papers, the Huntington Library, San Marino, California)

1894
Joined Coxey's Army, a protest march by unemployed workers from across the United States, and marched to Washington, DC. He left the march and became a hobo, traveling much of the US and Canada. He tramped to Niagara Falls and was thrown into the Erie County Penitentiary in Buffalo, New York, for vagrancy. He was sentenced to thirty days hard labor.

1895
Entered Oakland High School, where he wrote essays and short stories for the Oakland High School *Aegis*.

1896
Crammed for college entrance exams, working sometimes nineteen hours a day, and he joined the Socialist Labor Party. In September, Jack enrolled as a student at the University of California at Berkeley and stayed for one semester.

1897
Left the university due to a lack of financial resources. Jack corresponded through letters with his real father, W. H. Chaney, after the shock of learning John London was not his father. Jack now dove into a frenzy of socialist activity and writing. He wrote essays, poems, and short stories, all of which were rejected for publication. Then in July he set out on the steamship *Umatilla* to join the gold rush in the Klondike. Unknown to London, his stepfather, John London, died in Oakland on October 14, just after Jack reached Stewart Island above Dawson.

1898

Had to leave the Yukon because of illness (scurvy) and returned to Oakland. He began to write nineteen hours a day.

1899

Turned down a job at the United States Post Office so he could continue to write. It was Jack's busiest year. He wrote sixty-one new stories, jokes, poems, and essays, and made his first sale to *Overland Monthly*, with the story "To the Man on Trail." He quickly sold eight more stories to *Overland Monthly* for $7.50 apiece. Now he began to make his living at writing. He also got $120 from *The Atlantic*, America's premier literary magazine, for his story "An Odyssey of the North." This convinced him he could now compete with the best of them.

1901

Daughter Joan was born in January.

Jack London, writer, about 1903

(JLP 210, Jack London papers, the Huntington Library, San Marino, California)

1903

Birth father W. H. Chaney died on January 8.

1900

"An Odyssey of the North" was published in *The Atlantic*. Married Bessie May Maddern. About this same time, he met Charmian Kittredge, his future wife. He also published his first book, *The Son of the Wolf*, a collection of Klondike tales.

1902

Finished the first version (the one with the happy ending) of his classic story "To Build a Fire." Published his first novel, *A Daughter of the Snows*, which is set in the Yukon. He also sailed to England to research and write *The People of the Abyss*, a wonderful nonfiction account of the people and living conditions in the slums of the East End in London. For this book he went undercover, dressing and living like the people he wanted to understand. His second daughter, Bess, was born, and he started to write *The Call of the Wild* as a short story, but he couldn't find a place to stop, so it kept getting longer.

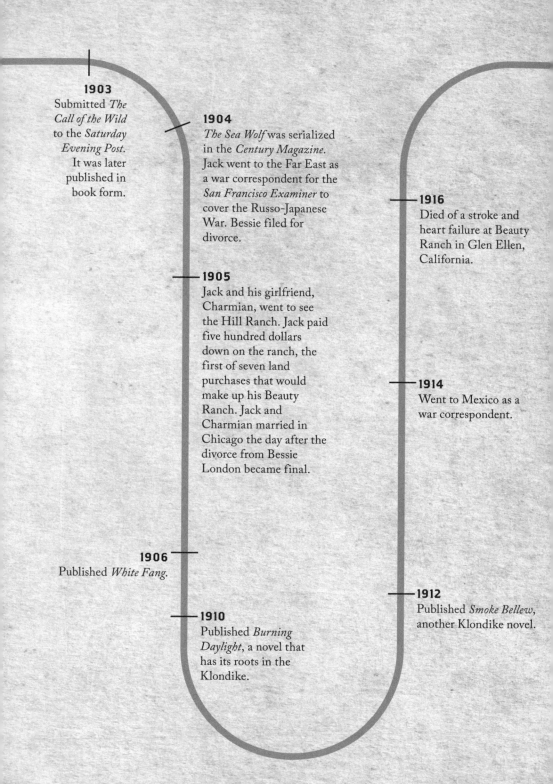

1903
Submitted *The Call of the Wild* to the *Saturday Evening Post*. It was later published in book form.

1904
The Sea Wolf was serialized in the *Century Magazine*. Jack went to the Far East as a war correspondent for the *San Francisco Examiner* to cover the Russo-Japanese War. Bessie filed for divorce.

1905
Jack and his girlfriend, Charmian, went to see the Hill Ranch. Jack paid five hundred dollars down on the ranch, the first of seven land purchases that would make up his Beauty Ranch. Jack and Charmian married in Chicago the day after the divorce from Bessie London became final.

1906
Published *White Fang*.

1910
Published *Burning Daylight*, a novel that has its roots in the Klondike.

1916
Died of a stroke and heart failure at Beauty Ranch in Glen Ellen, California.

1914
Went to Mexico as a war correspondent.

1912
Published *Smoke Bellew*, another Klondike novel.

GLOSSARY

Derived from the Klondike Glossary compiled by Scott Eckberg,
Park Ranger, National Park Service, Klondike Gold Rush
National Historical Park, Seattle Unit, 1986

http://www.nps.gov/klse/learn/education/upload/Glossary-2.pdf

Argonauts—Those who stampeded north to the Klondike were sometimes called Argonauts by the newspapers of the day, harkening back to the Greek heroes who accompanied Jason on his quest for the Golden Fleece.

bedrock—The hard rock or clay-packed underground surface on which placer gold eventually lodged. In the Klondike, this varied from ten to forty feet or more below the surface of the ground.

Bonanza King—A wealthy claim owner on Bonanza Creek; any of the wealthy claim owners in the Klondike (also called Eldorado Kings).

boom—Sudden success; the flourishing of a local economy following a gold strike or other such event.

break trail—To clear a trail with snowshoes, usually in advance of a dogsled.

cabin fever—The restlessness caused by spending a long, cold, and dark winter in close confinement.

cheechako—A newcomer who is ignorant of the terrain, the weather, the animals, the culture, and the necessary survival skills for the harsh Arctic winter ahead.

claim— Plot of land of authorized dimension registered for mining purposes and divided into bench, bar, and creek claims by geography.

colors—Traces or specks of gold remaining in the pan after panning.

cribbing—A structure of notched logs built log-cabin fashion and surmounted by a rope winch for raising pay dirt. The cribbing was usually built before excavation began and kept the growing dumps of pay dirt from seeping back into the shaft.

dogsled—Standard size was seven feet long, sixteen inches wide, and about seven inches high. Journalist Tappan Adney described one: "The bow is slightly upturned, and the top, of four longitudinal pine slats, rests upon four cross-frames of ash, with ash runners shod with two-inch steel shoes." They weighed about eighty pounds. "On it, lashed with thongs of moose-hide, were the food and gear for dogs and men."

drift—A tunnel excavated below a vertical shaft along bedrock to locate and remove pay dirt. In drift mining, the frozen ground is thawed in winter by fire (this process is also known as drifting). When a drift reaches fifteen to twenty feet, which is as far as profitable to drag the dirt, another shaft is sunk to meet and continue it.

Eldorado Kings—Any of the wealthy claim owners on Eldorado Creek; generically, any wealthy Klondike miner.

fool's gold—Iron pyrite, distinguished from true gold by its glittery hue and brittleness.

freeze-up—The time of year when the Yukon River freezes solid.

gold—Soft, yellow, corrosion-resistant, the most malleable and ductile metal, occurring in veins and alluvial deposits. The standard upon which the world's advanced national economies were based in the late nineteenth century.

Hän People, or Tr'ondëk Hwëch'in—An Athabascan people who speak the Hän language and live around the Klondike River.

King of the Klondike—Nickname of the wealthy claim owner and speculator Alexander "Big Alec" Macdonald, reputed to be the richest man during the Klondike boom, but who died broke.

Klondike fever—Gold fever. A great desire to get rich by prospecting for gold.

lining, or line down—To assist and control a boat over rough water by a line from the river shore.

miner's cabin—Small log cabin invariably found throughout the Klondike. Roughly twelve by fourteen feet, with walls six feet and gables eight feet high. The roof was heavily earthed; as a warm but rarely ventilated quarters, it was occupied by as many as four men at a time.

muck—The semifrozen mud just below the surface of the ground, "mucked out" with shovels.

mush, mushing—To travel with a dog team. Mushers are travelers using dog teams.

mush-ice—Soft ice just forming in a river approaching freeze-up, rapidly bringing all water transportation to a halt.

North West Mounted Police (NWMP)—A special constabulary created in 1873 by the Canadian government to establish and preserve the law in the Canadian West and thereby avoid the lawless condition of frontier settlement characteristic of the US West. The "Mounties" helped keep order during the Klondike Stampede. Today's descendant is the Royal Canadian Mounted Police.

oakum—A hemp used in rope making combined with pitch to caulk seams in boats—the oakum serving as binder.

outfit—One's entire supply of food and gear; the acquisition and purchase (outfitting) of supplies.

pan—To prospect with a gold pan.

pay dirt—The layer of soil/gravel which contains gold, hopefully in paying quantities, which has been removed to the surface in preparation for washing out.

pay streak—The ribbon of gold-laden soil deposited over geologic time, usually found at bedrock level and recovered by drifting. The source of pay dirt.

permafrost—In the northern regions of the planet, soil that is perpetually frozen.

placer—An alluvial or glacial deposit of sand or gravel containing particles of gold. In placer mining, one locates and works a placer claim, separating free gold from the uncovered or exposed pay streak by washing in pan, rocker, or sluice. Or dredge, a method developed after Jack's time in the Klondike.

Saint of Dawson—Jesuit priest William H. Judge, whose self-sacrificing assistance to stricken miners resulted in Dawson's first hospital and his own premature death.

sawpits—Raised platforms for supporting logs during whipsawing.

scurvy—A debilitating illness characterized by swollen gums and extremities, a yellowing of the skin, and pain in the joints. Untreated it leads to death. Causes are a lack of fresh fruit and vegetables and a vitamin C deficiency in the diet over a prolonged time.

shaft—Vertical tunnel excavated to bedrock, requiring up to two months' labor depending on the depth. A claim was usually "spotted" with shafts until the pay streak was located and drifting had begun.

sluice, sluicing—The separation of placer gold from lighter dirt and gravel by washing in sluice boxes (box sluicing) or in a trench cut into bedrock (ground sluicing). A sluice box is like a long tray that is open at both ends. Most will have riffles, spaced evenly along the length of the sluice, usually every few inches. Riffles cause small barriers to the water flow, which create eddies in the water, giving the heavier material (black sand and gold) a chance to drop to the bottom, behind the riffles.

Socialism—A political and economic system in which property and resources are owned or controlled by the public or the state. The term *socialism* also refers to any political or philosophical doctrine that advocates such a system.

sourdough—A longtime resident of Alaska or the Yukon, though after the Klondike Gold Rush, loosely applied to anyone who had lived through a far northern winter. Stemmed from the popularity in the Klondike of using sourdough as a leavening for bread instead of yeast or baking powder, which were less reliable in the harsh conditions.

Stampeder—Someone who leaves home to head for a rumored gold strike.

strike—A gold discovery.

sweep—A long pole-like oar used to rudder or steer a large boat or raft, located at the stern of the vessel.

sweeper—An overhanging tree branch along a river.

Tagish—A First Nations people who lived around Tagish and Marsh Lakes in the Yukon Territory of Canada during the gold rush. Tagish and Tlingit people from the coast have intermarried heavily. Members of the Tagish First Nation made the gold discovery that led to the Klondike Stampede—Keish (Skookum Jim Mason), Shaaw Tláa (Kate Carmack), and K̲áa Goox̱ (Dawson Charlie). Today, Tagish people live mainly in the Yukon towns of Carcross and Whitehorse.

Tlingit—An indigenous people of the Pacific Northwest coast of North America who traded with First Nations people of the interior by traveling over routes like the Chilkoot Trail. Tlingit traders would travel inland with dried fish and marine products to trade with interior First Nations for furs, clothing, and other goods. During the Klondike Stampede, Tlingit packers, along with the Tagish, charged for carrying supplies up over the summit of the Chilkoot and down to Lakes Lindeman and Bennett.

vein—A regularly shaped and lengthy occurrence of an ore.

whipsaw—The two-man saw used to cut planks from logs; also the act of using this saw—i.e., whipsawing.

Yukon stove—Perhaps one of the most valued fixtures of the Klondiker's outfit. Often one half of a sheet-iron barrel with a collapsible stovepipe. Sometimes a box made of sheet metal, with collapsible variations, taken north for cooking and heating. Although compact, one could cook and bake for a sizeable party with it.

JACK LONDON BIBLIOGRAPHY AND SOURCES

TAPED INTERVIEWS

Earle Labor in Shreveport, Louisiana

Dawne Mitchell in Dawson, Yukon Territory, Canada

David Neufeld in Whitehorse, Yukon Territory, Canada

Karl Gurcke, historian at the Klondike Gold Rush National Historical
  Park, Skagway, Alaska

WEBSITES

An all-around good site for Jack London information and writings:
  http://london.sonoma.edu

Jack London Museum (operated by the Klondike Visitors Association)
  in Dawson City, Yukon Territory, Canada:
  http://dawsoncity .ca /attraction/jack-london-museum/

Two sites devoted to Jack London's California ranch where he wrote
  many books, now a state historical park in Glen Ellen, California:
  http://www.parks.sonoma.net/JLPark.html
  http://www.jacklondonpark.com

BOOKS

Adney, Tappan. *The Klondike Stampede*. Vancouver, BC: University of
  British Columbia Press, 1994.

Berton, Pierre. *The Klondike Quest: A Photographic Essay 1897–1899*. Erin, Ontario, Canada: Boston Mills Press, 2005.

Dyer, Daniel. *Jack London: A Biography*. New York: Scholastic Inc., 2002

Haley, James L. *Wolf: The Lives of Jack London*. New York: Basic Books, 2010

Kingman, Russ. *A Pictorial Life of Jack London*. New York: Crown Publishers, 1979.

Labor, Earle. *Jack London: An American Life*. New York: Farrar, Straus and Giroux, 2013.

London, Charmian Kittredge. *The Book of Jack London* (two volumes). New York: The Century Co., 1921.

London, Jack. *The Call of the Wild, White Fang & To Build a Fire*. New York: Modern Library, 2002.

London, Jack. *The Portable Jack London* (Portable Library), edited by Earle Labor. New York: Penguin Books, 1994.

London, Jack, and Daniel Dyer. *The Call of the Wild: With an Illustrated Reader's Companion*. Norman, OK: University of Oklahoma Press, 1995

Morgan, Murray, and E. A. Hegg. *One Man's Gold Rush: A Klondike Album*. Seattle: University of Washington Press, 1972.

Neufeld, David, and Frank Norris, *Chilkoot Trail: Heritage Route to the Klondike*. Madeira Park, BC: Harbour Publishing, 2005.

North, Dick. *Sailor on Snowshoes: Tracking Jack London's Northern Trail*. Madeira Park, BC: Harbour Publishing, 2006.

Thompson, Fred. *To the Yukon with Jack London: The Klondike Diary of*

Fred Thompson, edited by David Mike Hamilton. Los Angeles: Zamorano Club, 1980.

Walker, Franklin. *Jack London and the Klondike*. San Marino, CA: Huntington Library Press, 1966.

Wilson, Mike. *Jack London's Klondike Adventure*. Hertfordshire: Wordsworth Publishers, 2000.

INDEX

(Page references in *italic* refer to illustrations.)